The Great
Power
Conflict

Key History for GCSE

The Great Power Conflict

Peter Fisher

Stanley Thornes (Publishers) Ltd

First published in 1998 by:
Stanley Thornes (Publishers) Ltd
Ellenborough House
Wellington Street
CHELTENHAM GL50 1YW
England

98 99 00 01 02 / 10 9 8 7 6 5 4 3 2 1

A catalogue record for this book is available from the British Library.

ISBN 0-7487-3370-1

For Jean, Ben and Kate

Printed and bound in China by Dah Hua Printing Press Co. Ltd
Designed by Hilary Norman
Illustrated by Hardlines
Cover photo: Corbis UK Ltd (front) · Sipa Press (back)
Picture research by Christina Morgan

Acknowledgements

With thanks to the following for permission to reproduce photographs and other copyright material in this book:

Associated Press 24;
Stringer/Associated Press 88;
Behrendt/De Telegraff, Amsterdam 90t;
Bilderdienst Suddeutscher Verlag 36;
Jim Borgman/Cincinatti Enquirer 70;
Jean-Loup Charmet 7;
Collections Musee Royal de L'Armee, Brussels 25;
Corbis UK 35b;
Express Newspapers/Historical Newspaper Service 34t;
Evening Standard 13;
Getty Images 6t, 27, 45, 60t;
'When the Wind Blows', Raymond Briggs, Hamish Hamilton, 1982 33;
The Independent 90b;
Krokodil/School of Slavonic and East European Studies, University of London 6b, 23;
Mark Riboud/Magnum 54;
Illingworth/Daily Mail/Solo Syndication 51;
NASA 35t, 92;
Peter Newark's Military Pictures 21;
'Vicky'/New Statesman 43b;
Popperfoto 30b, 43t, 44, 49, 56;
Rex Features 15, 34 (centre), 34b, 46, 47, 60b, 65, 67, 69, 71, 72, 73, 74, 76, 77, 79, 80, 82, 86, 87;
Norman Rockwell/The Four Freedoms/Imperial War Museum 10b;
Scott Camazine/Science Photo Library 30t;
Rosie Snell 93;
Frank Spooner Pictures 84;
News International/The Times – Ashley Coombes 85;
Topham Picturepoint 12, 17, 40, 53.

The publishers have been unable to trace the copyright holders of the following cartoons:

10t, 38, 39, 63, 68.

Should the publishers receive any information regarding the copyright holders they would be happy to make the necessary arrangement at the first opportunity.

The author would like to thank Dorothy Perriam for her help in preparing this book.

Every effort has been made to contact copyright holders. The publishers apologise to anyone whose rights have been inadvertently overlooked, and will be happy to rectify any errors or omissions.

Contents

1 Introduction to the Great Power conflict

Overview

▶ *How can you use sources to understand (and explain) the Great Power Conflict after 1945?*

One war ends

See Source **A**, May 1945. An historic moment. Having defeated Hitler, Allied troops from America and the Soviet Union meet for the first time. The Americans had fought across Western Europe. The Russians sweep across Eastern Europe. Within 14 weeks the Second World War ended, after America dropped two atom bombs in Japan. After 55 million deaths, the world looked forward to peace.

Another begins

It was not to be. The years after 1945 saw the world's two Great Powers, America and the Soviet Union, compete in a worldwide conflict. Between 1945 and 1991 this conflict, based upon rival systems of economics and government, split the world into two main power blocks. With the nuclear era as a background, the stakes could not be more deadly.

Differing viewpoints

This book is designed to help you to explain what happened and to understand reasons for the decisions made by the Great Powers, based upon how each felt, at the time, about the actions of the other. Throughout the book you will be asked to study a wide range of primary sources and, by asking questions, to turn them into evidence. One of the problems is that what each Great Power thought was happening was often more important than what was actually happening.

Look at Source **B**. It is a Soviet view of how they saw the spreading power of America after the Second World War. In it, the American government is shown as 'threatening' the Soviet Union by 'encircling' its borders with countries friendly with America. Drawn in the 1950s, Source **B** was published at the time

Source A East meets West: Torgau, Germany; May 1945

when the events were happening. This means it is a primary, or first-hand, source. It gives you ideas about how the Soviet Union felt, at the time, about the actions of America. From a study of primary sources you will see that America, the Soviet Union and Communist China, a third Great Power, often had different views of the same events. Looking at this evidence can help you understand the reasons for the Great Power conflict.

Source B A Russian view of American policy – grasping hands stretch out from the White House towards countries like Vietnam, Korea and Turkey

Source C A French cartoon showing the Russian leader, Stalin, spreading Communism through Eastern Europe after 1945

Study Source **C**. What can you learn from this primary source? It shows a Western view of the Soviet Union's actions after the Second World War. In American eyes, the Soviet Union seemed bent on spreading Communism across Europe.

Changes

When you were born, the Great Power conflict still held the world in its grip. Ugly symbols existed, such as the Berlin Wall. Now the Wall no longer exists except in the form of tourist souvenirs or museum exhibits (see page 80). Pulling the Wall down was a symbol of the totally unexpected changes in East–West relations. The 1990s saw the end of Communism, first in the Soviet Union which broke up into independent republics with free and democratic elections. These same reforms spread rapidly to many other countries in Eastern Europe, previously under the control of the Soviet Union. Because of these changes, a united Germany exists, formed from the two separate states of East and West Germany.

As the world heads towards the next millennium, the Great Power conflict seems consigned to a brief – but eventful – few decades of history.

Interpretations

In this book you are encouraged to make decisions and judgements by 'putting yourself in the shoes' of the people involved in the events described. You are also asked to think about the causes of events and the different motives for the Great Powers' actions.

To help you focus on the main ideas, you will be asked some key questions about different events and people. This means trying to interpret the events yourself, long after they have happened. You must make second-hand judgements. This process is similar to the way in which a historian might produce secondary evidence, long after the events, first by a study of the primary sources and then by interpreting the events.

You will find that parts of the book are arranged for class, group or individual work. All aim to help you enjoy your work and to develop your understanding of the conflict which divided the world for much of the past 50 years.

Questions

1 'Primary sources are always more reliable than secondary ones.' Is this true?

2 Study Source **A**. Consider ways in which this photo is: **a)** a useful source, and **b)** an unreliable source.

3 Choose either Source **B** or Source **C**.

a) Why might it not be wise to take the source at face value?

b) Upon which aspects of the Great Power conflict does it offer useful evidence?

4 What are some of the problems in studying the Great Power conflict?

The Great Powers

▶ *How did America and the Soviet Union compare as Great Powers?*
How were the two Great Powers different to each other?

Resources

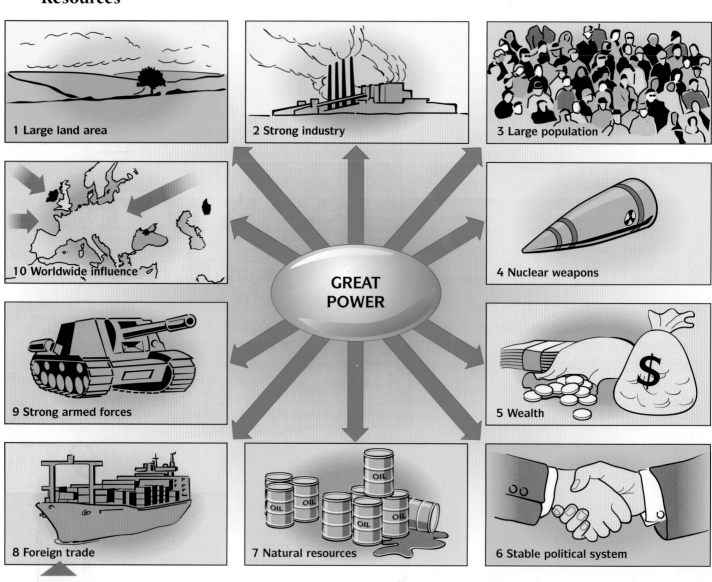

Source A Recipe for a Great Power

Source **A** shows what is needed to make a Great Power. The chart in Source **B** compares the key resources of America, the Soviet Union and China. Great Powers used their resources to influence other countries. They used their power to affect world events by persuading or forcing other countries to do as they wished. Often this led to conflict between

Great Powers, even if they themselves were not directly involved. After the Second World War the 'league table' of Great Powers was re-drawn. America and the Soviet Union stood out as clear leaders of the post-war world. In the Far East, China was soon to emerge as a Great Power.

Key differences

America and the Soviet Union were completely different in history and geography and, until 1991, in politics and economics.

America had a short history. Its geographical position made it secure, making the American people feel strong and safe. It had strong industries, efficient farming and much overseas trade. These things made America the richest country in the world.

The Soviet Union had a long history. Though huge in size, it had an unsafe Western border, across which many invaders had come. The Soviet Union was rich in natural resources but its industries and farms were not yet fully modernised.

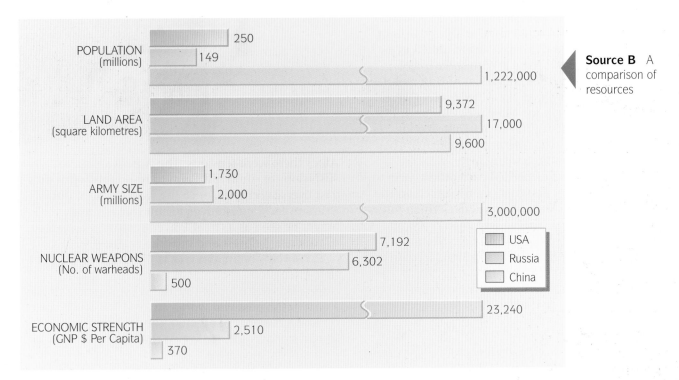

POPULATION (millions): USA 250, Russia 149, China 1,222,000

LAND AREA (square kilometres): USA 9,372, Russia 17,000, China 9,600

ARMY SIZE (millions): USA 1,730, Russia 2,000, China 3,000,000

NUCLEAR WEAPONS (No. of warheads): USA 7,192, Russia 6,302, China 500

ECONOMIC STRENGTH (GNP $ Per Capita): USA 23,240, Russia 2,510, China 370

Key: USA, Russia, China

Source B A comparison of resources

It was in politics and economics, until 1991, that the two countries differed most. Each had its own *ideology*, that is, its particular views on the best way to run the country. America's political system is based on *democracy*. It has a government chosen through free elections. America's economic system is called *capitalism*. All industry and land is owned by private individuals or businesses who try to make profits out of production.

The Soviet Union's ideology was based on *Communism*. In simple terms, this means that the good of the whole society should come before individual interests. So, for example, factories are owned by the state and not run for private profit. The Soviet Union's leaders decided that a strong Communist Party with tight control was vital to run the country; so until 1991 the Soviet Union was a one-party state. In the twentieth century the Soviet Union has modernised itself into a major world power.

Since 1949, China, the world's third Great Power, has had an ideology based on Communism. With its huge population, China has been concentrating on modernising its farming and building up its industries. With its vast resources, China has developed, in just five decades, into a major world power.

Questions

1 With a partner, list the 10 elements in Source **A** in your order of importance (1–10) for making a Great Power. Discuss the reasons for the order you have chosen.

2 Compare the strengths of America and the Soviet Union under the following headings:
  • geography;
  • economic power;
  • military power (see Sources **A** and **B**).

3 Study Sources **A** and **B**. Is it correct to regard China as a world power? What are China's strengths and weaknesses?

2 'Hot War' to Cold War

Uneasy allies

▶ *What tensions lay behind the show of wartime friendship?*
What needed to be sorted out in Europe after 1945?
Why did the wartime Allies fall out?

The Big Three

In Europe, from 1941 onwards, the Allies – Britain, America and the Soviet Union – were united in a common aim (see Source **A**). With three major powers fighting together, the defeat of Hitler's forces was just a matter of time. The Allied leaders were Winston Churchill (Prime Minister of Britain), Joseph Stalin (leader of the Soviet Union) and Franklin Roosevelt (the American President). They were known as the 'Big Three'.

The Allies knew they needed each others' help to defeat Hitler. Britain and America depended on the Soviet Union's Red Army to wear out German forces on the Eastern Front. The Soviet Union relied on British and American troops invading Western Europe. This would stretch the German forces in two directions. The Soviet Union's help would be needed to defeat Japan once Germany surrendered.

Allied tensions

Beneath this surface of friendship and cooperation all was not well. Disagreements amongst the Allies developed. They differed about how to win the war in Europe, and about how to keep the peace once the war was over. As well as this, there was suspicion caused by Communist and capitalist countries working together for the first time ever.

The Allies' main arguments arose over the 'Second Front' in Europe. In the West the 'D-day' landings did not take place until June 1944. By then, the Soviet Union had already been fighting off the German invasion for three years! Stalin was deeply suspicious of why the invasion was delayed for so long. Perhaps Stalin wondered whether America and Britain hoped to see Nazism and Communism destroy one another.

The Big Three: future aims

There was deep mistrust between the Americans and the Soviets because of their different *ideologies* (see page 9). Surprisingly, Roosevelt seemed to trust Stalin, but Churchill did not trust Stalin, and he had made his feelings clear. Even amongst the capitalist

Source A Hitler and Mussolini cower from the Allied 'thunderbolt'

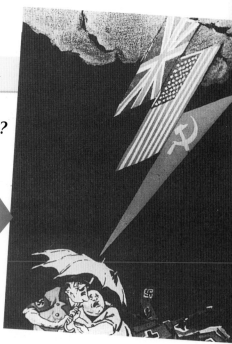

Allies there were tensions. The Americans were suspicious of Churchill's aim to re-establish Britain's vast overseas empire, once the war was over. But Britain's lack of resources meant that it could no longer be seen as a Great Power. Instead it remained as America's closest and most loyal ally.

Roosevelt's main aim was to end the war. He felt that discussions about lands captured from the Germans could wait, but he did want America to play a part in the post-war world. In 1941 Roosevelt spoke of the basic rights of all men, the *Four Freedoms*, shown in Source **B**. He hoped that the future would be based on such ideas.

Source B Painting by Norman Rockwell

Freedom of Speech

Freedom of Worship

Freedom from Want

Freedom from Fear

Stalin's main idea for the future was to protect the Soviet Union. Over 27 million citizens had died in the war.

Three times within his adult lifetime, Stalin had experienced attacks on his country from the West. He was determined that never again should the Soviet Union suffer a similar fate.

In spite of these disagreements, the war in Europe drew to a close in 1945. As American and Soviet soldiers met, the prospects for future friendship looked promising (see Source **C**).

Source C   Memories of a soldier from one of the first Soviet troops to meet American forces

We were like brothers ... we had defeated the enemy together ... we were united in fighting Fascism together ... the Americans gave us cigarettes, food, they gave us whatever they had, even watches ... the atmosphere was unbelievable ...

Lieutenant Alexander Silvashko, Soviet Army, 1945. From *The People's Century*, BBC, 1996

Source D   Memories of a soldier from the US Army

You must understand that we weren't really able to communicate with them except by sign language ... they were good people and we had no problem getting on with the individual Russian soldiers that we met there at all ... there was the relief that the war was drawing to a close and that the Allies had won the War ...

Lieutenant William Robertson, US Army, 1945. From *The People's Century*, BBC, 1996

Yalta

At a national level, the top priority was to sort out the future of Germany and its conquest in Eastern Europe. The 'Big Three' met at Yalta in the Soviet Union in February 1945. Surprisingly, perhaps, much was agreed (see below).

Chart showing results of the Yalta conference

The Allies agreed that:

- Germany was to be divided into four zones of occupation – one each for Britain, America, France and the Soviet Union (see page 18).
- Berlin was to be split up in a similar war (see page 19).
- Nazism was to be destroyed and its leaders tried for 'war crimes'.
- Germany was to pay *reparations* (compensation) for war damage (half of this to go to the Soviet Union).
- Countries in Eastern Europe were to have free elections.
- The Soviet Union was to declare war on Japan within three months.
- A United Nations Organisation should be set up to keep world peace in the future.
- On 7 May 1945 the German forces surrendered. The war in Europe was over, but in the Far East, Japan still fought on against the American and Commonwealth forces.

Questions

1   What do you understand by the following terms: Ally; Western Allies, Wartime Allies?

2   In what ways did the Allies rely upon one another from 1941–45?

3   Which of these factors do you think are the most important in causing the Wartime Allies to fall out?
   a) Basic differences in ideology.
   b) Disagreement about how to defeat Hitler.
   c) Mistrust among the Big Three leaders.
   d) Different experiences of direct warfare and suffering.
   e) Differing aims for the post-war world.
   f) Difficulties in sorting out post-war Germany.
   g) Difficulties between American and Soviet troops.

4   Sources **A** and **B** are both famous posters from the Second World War. Study each one. What theme or idea is common to both?

Origins of the Cold War

► *Why did the Cold War begin?*
Why did the Great Powers become rivals after 1945?
Which Great Power was most to blame for the outbreak of the Cold War?

Attitudes harden

As the Second World War ended, millions around the world looked forward to peace. A new worldwide peace-keeping organisation, the United Nations, was created (see Source **A**).

Harry Truman, America's new President, was aware that with their nuclear weapons America held the 'trump card' in Great Power relations. As a result their military forces were soon cut in numbers (see Source **B**).

Source A
Brave hopes for a peaceful world. Both America and the Soviet Union were members, but each viewed the future in different ways.

Source B
An ex-USAF pilot recalls

It was like a new life. Home … go back to see my girlfriend … plan for what we would do … back in the mountains of Utah … all the worry just gone … we disbanded the military very rapidly … now's the time for peace.

Lieutenant Gail Halverson. From *The People's Century*, BBC, 1996

Likewise, America's civilian population also looked forward to peace.

Source C   An American newsreel report

Shortly washing machines and other luxuries we've missed will be pouring from the factories at 1942 prices … and with new cars and new tyres on the way America will be rolling with a pre-war flourish. Yes, cars, radios, vacuum cleaners, nylons, juicy steaks – it sounds almost like a dream …

Extract from post-war cinema newsreel. From *The People's Century*, BBC, 1996

In contrast, the Red Army, six million strong, remained ready for war. Russia controlled 100 million East Europeans (see Source **B**, page 14). What was going on in Poland, Rumania, Hungary and Bulgaria? Was the defeat of Germany the first step in a plan to take over Europe?

As Britain and America became more and more worried about Stalin's motives, Winston Churchill wrote to the Americans to express concern (see Source **E**).

Source D   A Soviet soldier who served in Berlin in 1945 recalls his instructions

We were taught that the defeat of Fascism was an important step towards the victory of Socialism all over the world. Since the Red Army had liberated Eastern Europe sooner or later Socialism would be established. (In Berlin) … we were called in by our officers and told. 'Listen … the Germans were not solely responsible for this war, it wasn't just Hitler but the whole imperialist system … imperialism was responsible and who are the imperialists now? the same allies with whom we fought together against Hitler'.

Captain Anatoly Semiriaga, Soviet Army, Berlin, 1945. From *The People's Century*, BBC, 1996

Source E ►
Winston Churchill

The Soviet Union has become a danger to the free world. A new front must be created against her onward sweep. This front in Europe should be as far East as possible … A settlement must be reached on all major issues between the West and East in Europe before the armies of democracy melt.

Potsdam

The 'Big Three' met for the last time at Potsdam, near Berlin, in July/August 1945. Even before they met, Truman had made his views on the Soviet Union known (see Source **F**).

In the four months since Yalta, the 'Big Three' line-up had changed. Only Stalin remained. Churchill had lost power in Britain and had been replaced by Clement Atlee. Harry Truman, the new President, spoke for America. Stalin remained as secretive and determined as ever. Little was agreed. Relations between America and the Soviet Union got worse. After meeting Stalin, Truman wrote down his opinion of him.

Was Truman right to assume that the Russians were planning to conquer the world (Source **F**)? Or were the Soviet actions simply for Russia's self-defence, as Stalin had said? In the East, the Soviet Union stripped Germany of its industries. Millions of Germans were forced out of what now became Poland. Without agreement, the Russians pushed the Polish frontier westwards, deep into Germany, and set up a Communist government in Poland.

The Atom Bomb became a vital factor. Truman had kept news of the weapon from Stalin until 11 days before its use. America had made it clear that its secrets would not be shared. This increased Russian fears. Might the West attack to destroy Communism? A deadly new era dawned. It was called the *Cold War*.

The Cold War

The Cold War first developed in Europe – and in Germany in particular. It was a 'war' because it had two sides: America and her allies against the Soviet Union and her allies. It was 'cold' because there was no direct fighting. But all the other features of warfare existed. There were causes, armies, weapons, tactics, leaders, events and results. The world's two Great Powers feared each other. Each thought that the other wanted to destroy its way of life. This led to hostility, suspicion, quarrels, competition and threats. But neither side dared risk the prospect of 'hot' war.

During these years each side interpreted the other's actions in its own way. What one side saw as self-defence the other saw as aggression. Source **G** is just one example.

The Russians would soon be put in their place and the United States would then take the lead in running the world the way the world ought to be run.

A remark made by Truman in April 1945

The personal meeting with Stalin enabled me to see what the West had to face in the future. Force is the only thing the Russians understand. Stalin showed what he was after ... the Russians were planning world conquest.

A private note by Truman on Stalin and Soviet motives

Source F

This makes study of the Cold War difficult. Finding out what happened is easy enough. Working out the motives, or reasons, for the Great Powers' actions is more difficult. The very nature of the Cold War, with its climate of mistrust and suspicion, creates problems. What actually happened was often less important than what people at the time *thought* had happened!

BEHIND THE CURTAIN

SEE FOR YOURSELF. IS IT NOT OBVIOUS THAT THEY ARE "DEMOCRATIC GOVERNMENTS WHICH ENJOY THE CONFIDENCE OF THE OVERWHELMING MAJORITY OF THE PEOPLE OF THESE COUNTRIES"?

Source G
British cartoon showing a Soviet leader claiming that the countries of Eastern Europe had free elections after 1945

Questions

1 How does the evidence from Lieutenants Halverson (Source **B**) and Seminiaga (Source **D**) support Churchill's fears (in Source **E**)?

2 Were the Soviet Union's actions in Eastern Europe based on self-defence, or aggression? Give reasons for your answer.

3 Explain in your own words what is meant by the term 'Cold War'. Why, in many ways, was it similar to a 'Hot War'?

4 Which of the Great Power leaders, Truman or Stalin, was more to blame for the Cold War?

The Iron Curtain

Was Stalin justified in creating a 'buffer zone' in Eastern Europe?
Were the West right to regard Stalin's actions as a Soviet take-over of Eastern Europe?
How important was the Iron Curtain as a symbol of the Cold War?

'Liberation'

As the Soviet Red Army swept westwards, it 'liberated' the ancient capitals of Eastern Europe from Nazism.

Source A In Berlin, Ilsa Kruger – like millions of others – recalled her mixed feelings towards 'liberation'

What was to become of us? It was the Russians we were afraid of … we had to do what they told us.

Ilsa Kruger's testimony to the Cold War. From *The People's Century*, BBC, 1996

With Nazism destroyed, the big question was what would the Soviet Union do with the vast amounts of land, people and resources it now occupied?

Stalin's aim

Stalin was clear. The Soviet Union must be made safe from further invasions. After all, he reasoned, the Soviet Union had been attacked by Western powers three times within one generation: in 1914, 1922 and 1941! Hitler's recent attack had cost 27 million Soviet lives and had badly affected Soviet farms and factories.

In 1945 his opportunity arose, as his vast Red Army, six million strong, found itself controlling some 22 million citizens beyond the Soviet Union's pre-war boundaries. Between 1945 and 1947 the Soviet Union tightened its grip.

Source B Map showing the Soviet take-over of Eastern Europe, 1945–47

Legend:
— Iron Curtain
▨ Territory gained by USSR in 1945
☐ Countries under communist control
▩ Yugoslavia: communist but independent

0 km 500

The 'free elections' for Eastern Europe, agreed at Yalta, were held. One by one Communist parties came to power. The West thought that these elections were 'rigged' and suspected that the leaders of rival political parties were arrested and executed. Other non-Communist leaders, such as the Czech Jan Masaryk, met with mysterious 'accidents' or 'suicides'.

The Soviet Union said that the peoples of Eastern Europe had a democratic choice, and had chosen to elect Communist parties into power. Whatever the truth of the matter, the fact was that the Soviet Union – for the first time ever – had got a line of friendly countries across Eastern Europe; a 'buffer zone' of countries to protect her western border.

Source C Extract from Winston Churchill's 'Iron Curtain' speech, 5 March 1946

A shadow has fallen upon the scenes so lately lighted by the Allied victory. From Stettin on the Baltic, to Triest on the Adriatic, an Iron Curtain has descended across the continent. Behind that line … Communist parties, which are very small in all these eastern states, have been raised to power … all are subject to a very high measure of control from Moscow. This is certainly not the liberated Europe we fought to build up. Nor is it one which contains the essentials of permanent peace …

The Soviet Union's loss of life has been several times greater than that of Britain and America put together … So, what is so surprising about the Soviet Union, anxious for its future safety, trying to see that loyal governments should exist in these countries?

Source D Extracts from Stalin's reply to Churchill, 13 March 1946

Different opinions

Could the West have stopped this Soviet take-over of Eastern Europe?

President Truman, newly elected, was under pressure 'to bring the boys back home'. America had nuclear weapons, but what use were they? The people of Britain and America would not even consider another war. After all, Stalin and the Soviet Union had just been loyal Allies in the defeat of Hitler! There was nothing the West could do.

Stalin's actions were certainly watched with suspicion. Britain's ex-Prime Minister Winston Churchill warned of the dangers – as he saw them – in a famous speech on 5 March 1946 in America at Fulton, Missouri (see Source **C**).

Stalin's view understandably differed (see Source **D**). To Stalin, Churchill's speech seemed to threaten an Anglo-American alliance against the Soviet Union.

The Iron Curtain

The term 'Iron Curtain' was born. Was this a declaration of Cold War? Some thought so. Certainly Churchill hoped to alert the Americans to the Soviet control of Eastern Europe. But what were the Soviet motives? Were they, as Stalin had said, purely defensive? Or were they, as Churchill thought, a platform for future Soviet expansion? At first, the Iron Curtain was only 'a barrier of ideas'. It split Europe into a Communist East and a non-Communist West. It stopped cooperation and the exchange of information. At first, it did not stop the movement of people. A tidal wave of refugees flowed westwards.

Sealing the border

To start with, even in Germany, the Iron Curtain was just like any other frontier. Many people lived and worked in different zones.

In May 1952 Communist East Germany decided to block off its western border. Guards erected barbed wire and observation watch-towers along the border, for protection against 'spies, terrorists and smugglers' (see Source **E**).

The real reasons were different. First, East Germany was worried about the number of skilled workers fleeing to the West. Secondly, the East Germans were worried about the spread of non-Communist ideas into their 'workers' and 'peasants' state. Thirdly, the Communist East had become worried about the dramatic differences in standards of living emerging between East and West. Soon, the only safe – yet controlled – route between East and West was in Berlin; where the boundary stayed open.

For 44 years the Iron Curtain was an ugly scar cutting across Europe. It was the most visible sign of the division between East and West.

Source E An Iron Curtain watch-tower

uestions

1 Why did so many refugees flee from East to West?

2 Imagine how the following people might have reacted to the following events:
   a) Ilsa Kruger upon her 'liberation' (Source **A**).
   b) President Truman to Churchill's speech (Source **C**).
   c) Stalin to Churchill's speech (Source **C**).

3 Why do you think that Stalin created the Iron Curtain?

4 Were the main elements of the Iron Curtain, shown in Source **E**, built to protect the Soviet Union, or was Stalin set on future expansion?

Containment

► *What lay behind this American policy? How did 'Marshall Aid' support President Truman's doctrine?*

Post-war Europe

After the Second World War ended, President Truman visited Europe (Source **A**).

Even the victors, such as Britain, were close to economic ruin. In Eastern Europe, Stalin had already imposed Communism. To American eyes, an exhausted Europe looked vulnerable to a Soviet policy of expansion.

In 1947 Europe was still not free from war. In Greece a bitter civil war was raging, between the Royalists and the Communists. Britain tried to support the Royalists, but could not afford it. So Britain asked America for help. America had no obvious interest in Greece but saw a Communist threat there.

Elsewhere the Soviet Union was also putting pressure on Turkey. Communism was getting close to the Middle East, whose oil supplies were vital to the West. President Truman's advisers feared that if Greece fell to Communism, other countries in Western Europe – like Italy and France – might follow suit.

The Truman Doctrine

Truman decided to act. After a major speech he persuaded the US Congress to support Greece with 400 million dollars of military aid.

Source A
President Truman's impression of the destruction, summer 1945

> Ruined buildings, the never ending procession of old men, women and children ... wandering aimlessly, carrying, pushing and pulling their belongings. I was thankful that the United States had been saved the unbelievable devastation of this war.

Truman's speech became known as the *Truman Doctrine*. But what did it mean? Truman was openly critical of the way in which Communist Governments had been set up in Eastern Europe. He pulled no punches about what life was like for those living under Communist rule. By offering a stark choice, between Communism or non-Communism, his speech spelled out the reality of the post-war world. It meant that America was ready to take a major part in world affairs. For the first time ever America agreed to send money, weapons and advisors to any country, anywhere in the world, that felt threatened by Communism.

This led to the idea of America acting as the 'World's Policeman' against the threat of Communism. Truman's policy of holding back the spread of Communism was known as *Containment*. It became the backbone of American policy.

But in 1947 the Truman Doctrine was yet to be put to the test. Where would America's help first be sought? How could she act to protect the countries against the spread of Communism?

Marshall Aid

Two years on after the defeat of Hitler, much of Europe still lay at waste. Farms and factories produced less than they had before 1939. Even the weather was against recovery, with a severe winter in 1946–47 followed by floods and drought.

US General George Marshall visited Europe and recorded what he found (Source **B**).

Source B
A comment made by George Marshall in April 1947

> People crying for help, for coal, for food and for most of the necessities of life. The patient (*Europe*) is sinking.

Extracts from President Truman's speech to the US Congress, April 1947

- I believe it must be the policy of the United States to support free peoples who are resisting attempted subjugation by armed minorities or by outside pressure.
- ... the people of a number of countries ... have recently had totalitarian regimes (*Communist governments*) forced on them against their will.
- ... based on the will of a minority, forcibly imposed on the majority. (*It*) relies upon terror ... a controlled press ... fixed elections and the suppression of personal freedoms. (*He called upon*) nearly every nation ... to choose between alternative ways of life.

Might Western Europe fall to Communism? In June 1947 the Americans came up with the *Marshall Plan*. It offered American aid wherever it was needed.

Open to all?

Was the offer of aid open to all countries, even the Soviet Union? America said 'yes' but never seriously thought that the Soviet Union would accept (see Source **C**).

Stalin refused to allow any Eastern European countries to share in Marshall Aid, though some, like Czechoslovakia, had been keen to take part.

As Source **E** shows, Western Europe jumped at the American offer. Sixteen countries had drawn up the Organisation for European Economic Co-operation (OEEC) to distribute American aid. Over the next four years, 13 million dollars worth of food, fertilisers, vehicles and fuel flowed into Western Europe.

Source C President Truman announced America's idea

Our policy is directed not against any country or doctrine but against hunger, poverty, desperation and chaos ... Any country that is willing to assist in the task of recovery will find full cooperation (*from*) the US Government ...

Source D The Soviet attitude to the offer

Source E Welcoming Marshall Aid

Interpretations

Marshall Aid was the second half of Containment. By helping the recovery of Western Europe, Marshall Aid strengthened it against the threat of Communism.

As well as being a generous offer, there were strings attached to Marshall Aid. It was good for America, since it guaranteed export markets for goods made in American factories.

Marshall Aid became a vital, tactical weapon of the Cold War. Looking back, Truman later wrote, 'The Marshall Plan will go down in history as one of America's greatest contributions to the peace of the world ... without it, it would have been difficult for Western Europe to remain free from Communism.'

The Soviet view differed. They thought that the plan, 'widely advertised as a "plan to save peace", was aimed at uniting countries on an anti-Soviet basis ... a new alliance against Communism.'

Nowhere was the rising tension between the Great Powers more obvious than in an artificially divided Germany.

Questions

1 **a)** Which country in Europe suffered most from the war?
b) Compare the fortunes of America and the Soviet Union as a result of the war.

2 **Either** show Truman's idea of 'Containing Communism' by means of a diagram, **or** summarise, in your own words, what Truman meant in his April 1947 speech.

3 **a)** What point is the poster in Source **E** making?
b) Did all the Communist countries agree with this view?

4 **a)** Are the American and Soviet views of the Marshall Plan fair judgements, or are they *biased* (one-sided)? How helpful would such evidence be to an historian studying the Cold War?

3 Containment in action: Europe

The division of Germany

> *How did the former Allies try to help Germany?*
> *Why did their actions increase Great Power tensions?*
> *Why did Berlin become a flashpoint?*

Germany in 1945

Germany in 1945. A country with seven million dead, ruined cities and hungry, defeated, desperate people. In the Ruhr, police found a butcher's shop stocked with joints of human meat. Millions sought to make a 'new start' by becoming refugees.

Between 1945 and 1947, 16 million Germans arrived in Germany from Eastern Europe. One in eight (some two million) died. Many of their homelands were also in ruins. Factories were closed; industry was shattered. Farms could not grow enough to feed the people.

After the War ended the Allies stayed on and split defeated Germany into four zones.

Source B Map showing how Germany was divided

Berlin was divided up in the same way. Germany was run by an Allied Control Council, made up of army leaders. It would be one economic and political unit, with joint elections held in the four zones. The Allies hoped that, in time, Germany could be reunited into a 'safe' and democratic country. Such hopes were to be short-lived, for before long the wartime Allies fell out.

Issues

Reparations

The first clash occurred in 1946. It was over *reparations* (compensation). The Soviet Union wanted Germany to pay for the killing of 27 million Soviet citizens and widespread destruction it had caused in the war. Stalin wanted 10 million dollars from Germany. At Potsdam the Allies agreed that the Soviet Union should be given a quarter of the industrial goods made in the Western zones, in return for food and coal from the Soviet zone. The Soviet Union was also allowed to strip the factories in the Soviet zone and send their machines to the Soviet Union.

The British and Americans sent the industrial goods to the Soviet Union, as agreed. But Russia failed to send back food and coal. So in May 1946 the

Source A The *Guardian* newspaper reported on Germany's problems, November 1945

Millions of Germans are on the move. Groups trek hundreds of miles and lose half their numbers through disease and exhaustion. Children have arrived in Berlin looking like the emaciated (starved) creatures of Belsen (a Nazi concentration camp).

British and Americans stopped sending industrial goods to the Soviet zone.

Economics

More problems faced Britain and America. Should they continue to pay for food for people in the Western zones in years to come? Or should the German farms and factories be built up? The Western Allies decided to build up their German zones. Stalin – deeply suspicious of a fresh and strong Germany – watched with mistrust.

Administration

First, in January 1947, the British and American zones were joined together. Later, in June 1948, the French zone was added, to form one Western zone. Again, Stalin watched these events with mistrust. The Soviet Union forced its Eastern zone of Germany to accept the Communist way of life. In contrast, in the Western zone elections, the Communists never gained much support.

Crisis in Berlin

Location

After 1945, over two million Berliners found themselves in a unique position. Like the rest of Germany, the city was split into four sectors (see Source **D**).

Yet Berlin lay 100 miles (62.5 km) within the Soviet zone. To protect Berlin, free 'access rights' using agreed roads, rail, canal and air routes existed across the Soviet zone to allow the movement of people and goods between the Western sectors and the Western zones of Germany. Western Berlin stood out as an 'island of capitalism' surrounded by Soviet controlled Communists.

Survival

To ordinary people, such matters of politics and ideology mattered little. Those who survived faced the twin tasks of survival and rebuilding.

Source C Ilsa Krüger recalls taking a direct part in rebuilding the devastated city

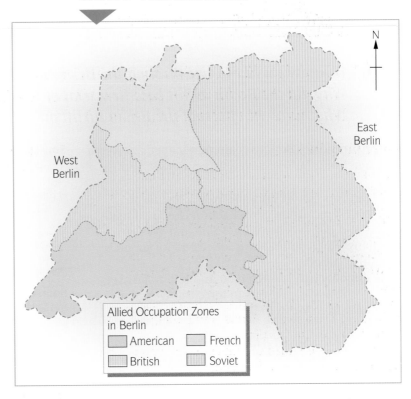

Source D Allied zones in Berlin

> Our beautiful city was flattened. We took picks and hammers, anything we could get hold of. We cleared up the bricks and then we formed up a great long line, passing them from hand to hand …
>
> From *The People's Century*, BBC, 1996

Allied action

As the Great Power conflict grew, Stalin worried about the motives of the West. What were their plans for a post-war Germany?

The final straw came when the Soviet Union learnt of Allied plans to introduce a new currency. This was intended to help unite the Western zones and strengthen Germany's economy.

Soviet reaction

Stalin was angry. Vulnerable Berlin and its isolated population would be the first pawns in a game of Great Power chess, using 'Cold War' style rules.

In 1948 the Soviet Union began to make Western access by road and rail to Berlin more and more difficult. Then, in June, the Soviet Union cut off Berlin from Western Germany. The Berlin Blockade had begun.

1 How might Ilsa Krüger feel about Soviet actions in June 1948 (Source **C**)?

2 Were Stalin's fears about the Allied actions to rebuild Germany justified?

3 News of the Soviet Blockade has just broken. You must advise President Truman how to react. The possible options open to the Allies are set out below:
   a) do nothing;
   b) protest to the Soviet Union;
   c) protest to the United Nations;
   d) use the Soviet actions as propaganda against Communism;
   e) send in the US army;
   f) threaten the Soviet Union with nuclear weapons;
   g) use the atomic bomb on the Soviet Union;
   h) supply the Western Berliners with supplies by air.

   Discuss them in a small group. What advice would you offer to the President? Consider what the effects of your advice might be.

Blockade and airlift

► **What was it like to live through the Berlin airlift?**
Why did the Berlin airlift become a trial of Great Power strength?
What were the effects of the Berlin airlift on Germany and on Great Power relations?

On 23 June 1948, Berlin's main newspaper received a message from the Soviet News Agency (see Source **A**).

Berlin was cut off from the West. 'Technical difficulties' meant the Soviet Union closed all roads, canals and railways between Berlin and Western Germany. For good measure, all electricity supplies were also cut off.

Berlin only had enough food and fuel to last six weeks. The Soviet aim was to force the West to withdraw from Western Berlin by reducing its population to starvation.

This was the Soviet Union's first direct challenge to the American idea of 'Containment'. America's leaders were united in opposition (see Sources **C**, **D** and **E**).

Source C   General Clay, US Commander, in Berlin

When Berlin falls, Western Germany will be next. If we withdraw our position in Berlin, Europe is threatened … Communism will run rampant.

Source D   President Truman

We are going to stay, period.

Source E   General Marshall

We stay in Berlin. We will supply the city by air.

Captain Gail Halverson was one American pilot who volunteered in response to General Marshall's order (see Source **F**).

Source F   Captain Gail Halverson

A telex came in … we want four of your aeroplanes to leave Mobil, Alabama and go to Frankfurt within four hours … so I volunteered. We knew the dire straits that the people of Berlin were under.

Source A   Message from the Soviet News Agency, 23 June 1948

The Soviet administration is compelled to halt all traffic to and from Berlin tomorrow at 0600 hours because of technical difficulties.

Source B   A Soviet officer in Berlin recalls what lay behind the Soviet actions

The blockade was prepared weeks in advance … we'd done everything we could to persuade the Allies to leave West Berlin. We decided to force them to leave by making life intolerable for West Berliners.

Major Anatoly Semiriaga. From *The People's Century*, BBC, 1997

Britain and America decided to *airlift* supplies into Berlin along three narrow air corridors through the Soviet zone (see Source **G**).

Source G   Agreed air corridors to Berlin

The first flight, on 26 June, brought in 80 tons of milk, flour and medicine. By September, heavily laden transport aircraft were landing in Berlin every three minutes – day and night as in the photograph in Source **H**.

The Berliners became desperate. By October they were allowed only small amounts of fat, spam (tinned ham), potatoes and bread.

Berlin's 2.1 million people needed 4,000 tons of supplies a day to survive. By Spring 1949, 8,000 tons were being flown in each day. In all, 2 million tons of supplies were flown in.

The Soviet Union tried to stop the airlift. They 'jammed' the airwaves used by Allied pilots. They 'shadowed' Allied flights with Soviet fighter aircraft to make sure they stayed within the air corridors. But, why didn't they stop the airlift through direct action?

To stop the airlift inside the agreed 'Air Corridor' Russia would have had to shoot down Western planes. But Stalin was frightened of America's nuclear weapons. On 12 May 1949, after 11 months, the blockade was lifted.

The blockade: whose fault?

What did the leaders of the Great Powers make of the blockade?

Both America and the Soviet Union had different versions of the motives behind the Berlin blockade (see Sources **J** and **K**).

Source H
Templehof was the key airport in the American sector of Berlin. This photograph shows German children watching an American cargo plane land.

Source I
Captain Gail Halverson remembers his 24-hour routine:

We'd fly all night and come back in the middle of the day … sleep six hours and take off again … around the clock.

From *The People's Century*, BBC, 1997

Source J   President Truman's version was as follows

When we refused to be forced out of Berlin, we demonstrated to Europe that we would act when freedom was threatened. This action was a Russian plan to probe the soft spots in the Western Allies' positions.

Source K   The Soviet version

The crisis was planned in Washington, behind a smoke-screen of anti-Soviet propaganda. In 1948 there was the danger of war. The conduct of the Western powers risked bloody incidents. The self-blockade of the Western powers hit the West Berlin population with harshness. The people were freezing and starving. In the Spring of 1949 the USA was forced to yield … their war plans had come to nothing, because of the conduct of the Soviet Union.

Whatever the cause, the effects on Germany, and on relations between the Great Powers, were of vital importance.

So ended the first struggle of wills between East and West. The tactics were designed not to kill, but to threaten. This set the pattern for future Cold War conflicts.

Questions

1 a) What was the Soviet aim in imposing the blockade?
b) Why were the Western Allies unwilling to give Berlin up?

2 Why did the Soviet Union fail to stop the airlift of supplies to Berlin?

3 How is the American version of the blockade (Source **J**), different from the Soviet view (Source **K**)?

4 Which power bloc – East or West – was most to blame for the Berlin blockade?

5 Explain why the Berlin blockade was lifted.

Reaction to the crisis: NATO and Warsaw Pact

▶ **What were the short- and long-term effects of the crisis in Berlin?**
Can 1949 be seen as a watershed in Great Power relations?
Were the Great Powers justified in creating two new military alliances?

NATO

Even before the Berlin crisis ended, America was convinced that a wide-ranging and strong military alliance was needed. In 1948 five West European countries had signed the Brussels Treaty. This included an agreement to give each other military aid in the event of armed aggression.

The Soviet Union's leaders made no secret of their views concerning America's motives.

On 4 April 1949, the North Atlantic Treaty was signed in Washington, USA. NATO had an original membership of 12: Britain, France, Belgium, Holland, Luxembourg, Portugal, Denmark, Ireland, Italy, Norway, Canada and the USA. Later members were Greece and Turkey, who joined in 1952, and West Germany, which joined in 1955. Source **B** shows their location.

NATO consisted of several key aspects (see below).

Source A
Communique from the Soviet Foreign Ministry, 29 January 1949

The ruling circles of the USA and Britain have in the past two months been engaged in setting up a North Atlantic Alliance. It is easy to see that these aims are closely interwoven for the establishment of Anglo-American world supremacy, under the leadership of the USA.

Source B NATO members in the Northern Hemisphere

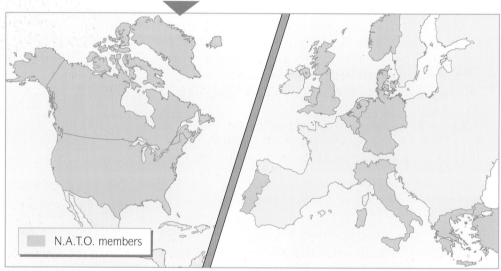

N.A.T.O. members

Key features of NATO

- The alliance was designed to be purely defensive'.
- All members agreed to regard an attack on any one of them as an attack on all of them.
- All agreed to place their defence forces under a joint NATO command.
- NATO Command would coordinate the defence of the West.
- America was NATO's strongest member by far.
- America agreed – for the first time ever – in advance, to go to war on another country's behalf.

Reactions to NATO

The Soviet Union saw NATO as an attempt to 'encircle' their nation with countries hostile to Communist ideas, and made official protests.

After the recent events in Berlin, the peoples of Western Europe were only too glad to take refuge in an alliance backed up with the vast military strength of the USA. Ernest Bevin, Britain's Foreign Minister, voiced the thoughts of millions (see Source **C**).

Like others, my country has had forced upon it the task of fighting two world wars against aggression within a quarter of a century. Today will bring a feeling of relief. At last democracy is no longer a series of isolated units.

Source C Ernest Bevin

A second Super Power

On 23 September 1949, the West woke up to a shock. Years ahead of predictions, the Soviet Union announced that it had successfully exploded its first nuclear bomb. Stalin's aim to develop a Soviet bomb at breakneck pace had paid off. East–West relations entered a deadly new phase.

Changes in Germany

The Berlin crisis also led to important political changes. The aim of German unification agreed at Potsdam only four years earlier was in tatters. Each side accused the other. The West claimed that only Russia's refusal to permit free elections prevented complete German unification. The East claimed that the West had broken the Potsdam agreement by separating off their three zones.

It was now clear that Germany could not be united. The process of creating two separate German states was speeded up.

In August 1949 the German Federal Republic (West Germany) came into being. Its territory was based on the three occupation zones controlled by the Western Allies. Bonn became its capital city. Dr Konrad Adenauer became its first Chancellor (Prime Minister).

In September 1949, the Soviet Union responded by re-naming their zone of Germany the German Democratic Republic (East Germany). Berlin itself also became split into two halves: West and East.

Soviet reaction

The Russians viewed the creation of West Germany as another step towards rebuilding a strong, aggressive, anti-Russian state. Source **D** shows Russia's long-standing fear. In 1955 Russia's worries increased when the new West Germany was allowed to join NATO.

The Warsaw Pact

In Soviet eyes, the events justified the need to create a counter military force (see Source **E**).

Source D Nazi aggression 'hatching out' of rebuilt West Germany

This treaty became known as the Warsaw Pact.

Between 1949 and 1989, NATO and the Warsaw Pact acted as the umbrellas for collective defence of the West and East. However, as pages 90–91 show, the issue of an expanded NATO remains of concern to the current leaders of the Great Powers.

Source E
Extract from communique establishing the Warsaw Pact

> 14 May, 1955.
> In accordance with the pact of friendship, co-operation and mutual assistance between the People's Republic of Albania, the Hungarian People's Republic, the USSR and the Czechoslovak Republic, the states have decided to set up a unified command of armed forces ...

Questions

1 a) Why was NATO set up?
b) Why did America want to join the new alliance?
c) What was the Soviet Union's reaction to NATO?

2 What reasons did East and West give for the failure to unify Germany?

3 Why was the Soviet Union worried about West Germany joining NATO? How did the Communist countries react (Source **E**)?

4 Why has the enlargement of NATO created difficulties in recent Great Power relations (see pages 90–91)?

4 Containment in action: the Far East

China 1949–50

▶ *How did the Communist take-over of China change the balance of Great Power relations?*
How did Mao's and Stalin's views of Communism differ?
How did each Great Power react to the emergence of Communist China?

Background

China: a vast nation – both in area and population. Once, China had been an important power in the Far East. By 1900 it had become weak, backward and inward-looking. Between 1900 and 1950 the Chinese people faced serious problems (see below).

China's problems

Trade European powers such as Britain exploited the country's trade.

Industry Few industrial areas. Little mechanisation.

Food supply Frequent famines caused by drought or floods.

People A massive peasant population – very few able to read or write.

Farming Backward. Little progress in farming methods. Mostly 'subsistence level' (peasants produced just enough to survive).

Government Nationalist government in power, led by Chiang Kaishek. A corrupt and inefficient government. Few reforms.

Source A Mao Zedong

We proclaim the establishing of the PRC (People's Republic of China). Our nation will enter the family of peace-loving nations of the world. It will promote world peace and freedom. Our nation will never again be an insulted nation. We have stood up. Our revolution has gained the sympathy of the masses through the entire world.

Source B Mao Zedong, 1 October 1949

Despite these problems a country of China's size, population and potenial could not be ignored. America and the Soviet Union both played a part in the struggle for power in China between the non-Communist Nationalists and the Communists. In this way, the focus of America's and the Soviet Union's Cold War spread from Europe to the Far East.

Throughout the 1930s and 1940s, America backed Chiang Kaishek, the Nationalist leader. His forces were kept in power with American money, arms and advisors. The Americans believed it was vital to stop Mao Zedong's Communists gaining power.

At first, Mao Zedong looked to Moscow for help. Stalin thought that China's Communist Revolution should be like the Soviet one of 1917. It should be based upon the support of factory workers in towns. But China was nothing like the Soviet Union. Instead, Mao decided to gather his support from the millions of peasants in the countryside.

In the 1920s and 1930s the Nationalists and Communists fought out a bitter civil war. Between 1937 and 1945 the two sides joined together to fight the Japanese. After the Second World War America tried to keep the two sides together, with Chiang Kaishek in charge. But this attempt failed and a brutal civil war broke out again.

On 1 October 1949 Mao Zedong made an announcement (see Sources **A** and **B**).

The Communist victory surprised the whole world. Even the Soviet Union had thought that Mao's Communists had little chance of winning power.

American reaction

The Communist success came at the height of the Cold War. To America it seemed that Mao's victory was masterminded by Moscow, as part of the Communist struggle for world conquest. Might other poor countries follow China's example and set up Communist governments – in South East Asia; the Middle East; South America; Africa? America was certain that 'containment' must now become a worldwide idea.

To America, the 'loss' of China was a disaster. Chiang Kaishek was forced to flee to the small island of Formosa (now called Taiwan). He was bitter at his defeat, and very critical of American support for his Government during the Civil War. He described the Communist Government as 'a puppet directed by Moscow' and Mao Zedong as 'the Number One traitor in Chinese history'.

America refused to recognise the Communists as the legal government of China. When Mao threatened to invade Formosa, the American Seventh Fleet protected Chiang Kaishek's exiled forces. At the UN America supported Chiang Kaishek's right to keep the China seat. In 1950 America banned all trade and travel links with China. For the next 20 years America tried to freeze Communist China out of world affairs.

Soviet reaction

The Soviet Union welcomed Mao's success as a victory for 'World Communism' and a major step towards the spread of 'World Revolution'.

Source C Poster illustrating Sino-Soviet friendship

СЛАВА ВЕЛИКОМУ КИТАЙСКОМУ НАРОДУ,
ЗАВОЕВАВШЕМУ СВОБОДУ, НЕЗАВИСИМОСТЬ И СЧАСТЬЕ!

Mao went to Moscow for talks with Stalin. In February 1950 the two countries signed a 'Treaty of Friendship' which was meant to last for 30 years. The Soviet Union agreed to supply China with loans, military aid and technical help to develop China's industry.

At the United Nations, the Soviet Union backed Communist China's claim to take over the 'China' seat still held by the Nationalists, but America would not agree. In protest, the Soviet Union walked out of the UN.

A third Super Power

America and the Soviet Union both failed to realise the potential power of China and the influence of Mao. Stalin saw Mao as a junior partner. America saw Mao as Stalin's puppet. Both were wrong.

The Chinese Revolution gave hope to millions of poor people in Third World countries all over the world. It would be Mao, not Stalin who would lead this new breed of Communism. Sooner or later Stalin and Mao would fall out. As friends or enemies, the Soviet Union and America would have to take notice of the new Red Star in the East.

In 1948 Nationalist China's representative at the United Nations issued some prophetic words (see Source **D**).

Source D Extract from Nationalist China's representative to the United Nations, New York, 1948

> The fate of the entire Far East is linked to that of China. Because the Chinese Communists will help Communism in all the Far East. Against this tide, you have built up in the West a solid dyke. But now, this tide will overflow in another direction.

An Eastern version of Europe's iron curtain was being created: a 'bamboo curtain'. Soon China would flex her military might. How would the Great Powers react?

Questions

1 Why did America support Chiang Kaishek before 1949?

2 a) What does Source **C** suggest about the relationship between the Soviet Union and China?
   b) Why might the Soviet Union want to depict the relationship like this?

3 a) Why was Stalin pleased to support Mao from 1949?
   b) Why might the Soviet and Chinese views of Communism lead to future differences?

The Korean War

> *Why did Korea become a Cold War flashpoint?*
> *How did the War put 'Containment' to the test?*
> *How did Korea reveal the limits of a Great Power's influence?*

38° North

Since 1910 Korea had belonged to Japan. When the Second World War ended in 1945, the Allies agreed that Korea should become an independent country. Japan surrendered to Soviet forces in the north of Korea, and to American forces in the south. A temporary dividing-line was drawn up along the 38th parallel of latitude (38° North). Later, it was intended that Korea should hold free elections and be reunited.

As the Cold War developed in Europe, the division between North and South Korea became deeper. Although the Soviet Union and America had withdrawn their forces they continued to provide support – the Soviet Union to the North, America to the South. All attempts to unite the country failed. In 1948 two separate countries were set up. North Korea had a Communist government, led by Kim Il Sung. In South Korea a non-Communist state was formed, under Syngman Rhee.

The Chinese Revolution in October 1949 meant that now North Korea had two friendly Communist giants on its northern border.

Why war?

On 25 June 1950 North Korean forces armed with Soviet weapons crossed the 38th parallel and invaded South Korea. The table below suggests possible reasons why the war began.

Phase One

In just three days they had captured Seoul, the capital of South Korea (see Source **A**).

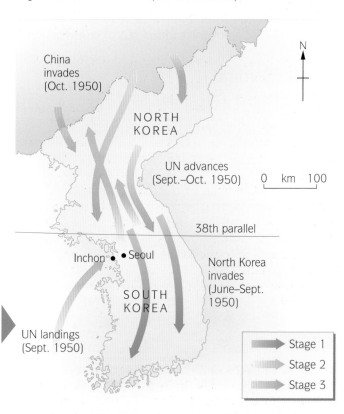

Source A   Map of Korea

Was this the first armed attempt towards the Soviet aim of world domination? The West certainly thought so.

Possible causes of the Korean War	
Was it:	*Reason:*
A show of Soviet strength towards the Americans – part of the Cold War?	To get their own back after the 'climb down' over Berlin?
A show of Soviet strength towards the Chinese?	Stalin showing Mao that he was the leader of Communism in Asia?
A North Korean attack planned in Moscow and backed by Peking?	It would strengthen the Soviet Union's defences in the Pacific (America thought this was the reason)?
An independent attack by North Korea, without Soviet or Chinese backing?	Because America had not included Korea in her defence plans for the Pacific?
An attack provoked by South Korea?	To regain American help against Communism (North Korea claimed that South Korean troops had attacked first)?

America acts

To prevent the fall of South Korea, America had to act. Containment was called for.

President Truman saw the North Korean invasion as part of a Communist plot (see Source **B**).

Truman moved quickly. He sent the US Seventh Fleet to strengthen Formosa (Taiwan) against possible Chinese attack. He ordered the war hero, General MacArthur, to go to Korea with military supplies.

An American motion was passed at the United Nations demanding that the North Koreans should withdraw from South Korea. Then, on 27 June, America put forward a second motion to the United Nations' Security Council. The UN agreed (see Source **C**).

America was only able to gain this UN backing by chance. When the Korean War began, the Soviet Union were *boycotting* (deliberately absent from) the UN Security Council. This was in protest at America's treatment of Communist China. When the UN Security Council agreed to America's demands, there were no Soviet leaders present to *veto* (stop) the decision.

The UN called upon its members to provide military forces. America's new NATO allies felt they must support America in the Far East, in return for US support in Europe. By this time, America was already involved in the Korean War. US troops formed the bulk of the UN forces, and General MacArthur was Commander-in-Chief of the whole operation.

Phase two

As UN forces built up in South Korea, the Communists pressed on to capture Pusan (see Source **A**). On 15 September, MacArthur's forces landed at Inchon (Source **D**) to attack North Korean supply routes from the rear.

Bitter fighting followed. Eventually the UN forces captured Seoul. By October 1950 the North Koreans had been forced back behind the 38th parallel. Communism had been contained, so was the UN's task over? Should the Americans stop there?

Phase three

The Americans did not think so.

> Here in Asia is where the Communist conspirators have elected to make their play for global conquest. If we lose the War to Communism in Asia, the fall of Europe is inevitable. There is no substitute for victory.

Source E The American General MacArthur's feelings

Source B Extract from speech made by President Truman

> The attack upon Korea makes it plain beyond all doubt that Communism has passed beyond the use of subversion to conquer independent nations and will now use armed invasion and war.

Source C UN Security Council

> To furnish such assistance to the Republic of Korea as may be necessary to repel the armed attack and to restore peace and security in the area.

Source D American assault craft

MacArthur and Truman saw this as the chance to unite Korea. Not content with containment, they wanted to free North Korea from Communist control.

China saw the American plans as a real threat. If UN forces captured North Korea, they might press on to attack the border with China. And they could use North Korea as a base for bombing raids on Chinese industry.

> If the Americans cross the 38th parallel, China will be forced to intervene in Korea.

Source F The Chinese issued a warning

Despite this warning, Truman ordered MacArthur to cross into North Korea on 7 October. He asked for UN support for this action, and got it. The UN forces advanced and captured the North Korean capital. Then they continued north, towards the Chinese border. Would China carry out its threat?

China acts

October 1950. Three hundred thousand Chinese troops crossed the Yalu River (the border between China and North Korea, see Source **A**). They were to fight alongside the North Koreans as 'Chinese People's Volunteers'. They were called 'volunteers' so that China would not have to declare war on the UN forces. Officially, the Korean War was still a Civil War between the South (with UN backing) and the North. In reality, it had become a Great Power Conflict between America (and its allies) and the Chinese Communists, who were supported by Soviet weapons and advisors.

The massed Chinese armies met the UN forces and pushed them back through sheer weight of numbers. In two weeks the UN forces lost all of North Korea. By January 1951 they had been forced to retreat beyond the 38th parallel.

In February, after bitter fighting, MacArthur managed to push the Chinese back to the 38th parallel again. Losses on both sides were heavy.

President Truman was keen to set up a cease-fire along the 38th parallel, but MacArthur pressed on into North Korea. He wanted to extend the war into China itself and to defeat Mao Zedong, with the aid of Chiang Kaishek's forces. He even suggested using America's nuclear weapons against the Chinese.

But Truman was determined that the Korean War should not develop into a full-scale Asian War. Then came some shock news (see Source **G**). Many Americans still felt that MacArthur was right. But the American Secretary of State felt that the risks were too great (see Source **H**).

Truman, though unpopular, stuck with his policy of containment. The war had reached 'stalemate'. The two sides had dug themselves into a maze of trenches and fortifications on opposite sides of the 38th parallel. In the air, there were 'dog fights' between American and Chinese pilots, who were in Soviet jets. American bombers pounded military targets in North Korea.

Peace, but problems

At the suggestion of the Soviet Union, peace talks began at Panmanjom in June 1951. All hopes of winning the war, or of uniting Korea, had now vanished. The talks were complex, and often broke down. Meanwhile the war dragged on, with each side using words as well as weapons. Source **I** is a typical example of such propaganda.

In November 1952, General Dwight Eisenhower replaced Truman as America's President. Eisenhower wanted to end the war. He tried to pressurise the Chinese into a truce, but the fighting went on. In

Source G *Evening Standard*, London, 11 April 1951

> President Truman has dismissed seventy-one-year-old General Douglas MacArthur from all his posts.

> Against the advantages of spreading the war to the mainland of China, there must be a risk of Soviet intervention and of World War III.

Source H The American Secretary of State

> It has been charged that the forces in Korea are engaged in a pointless struggle. Nothing could be further from the fact. Their gallant, determined and successful fight has checked the Communist advance. They have administered terrible defeats to the Communist forces.

Source I Extract from a speech made by the American Secretary of State

1953 Stalin died. China could not be sure that the Soviet Union would continue to provide help and supplies. So China agreed to peace talks. An armistice was signed on 17 July 1953, but no peace treaty could be agreed. It took over 30 years to finally resolve all the issues caused by the war.

The effects of the war

The Korean War was the first war between East and West, and the second crisis of the Cold War. This time, all the Great Powers wanted to limit the war to Korea. Although none of them won, the real loser was Korea itself (see balance sheet opposite).

By the end of the war, East and West were even more hostile towards each other.

With the Soviet Union now able to threaten with its own nuclear weapons, all future Great Power affairs would be acted out with the stakes raised so high as to threaten the end of humanity.

The lessons of Korea

Both Great Powers learnt lessons from the Korean War. The Soviet Union and America knew that China would act if threatened by the West.

The Korean War: a balance sheet

	Gains	Losses
Korea	None	• Casualties (dead and wounded) • 1.3 million South Korean (military) • 520,000 North Korean (military) • Over three million civilians • Much industry destroyed • Agriculture ruined • Millions of refugees
UN	• Gained respect by taking prompt, direct action. • Used combined force to stop aggression. • Achieved joint action by members	• 17,000 casualties • Conduct of war almost entirely controlled by US • Decisions weakened by power of veto
America	• Saved South Korea from Communism • Containment policy seen to work against Asian Communism	• 42,000 casualties • Defence spending went up from 12 to 60 billion dollars • Failed to liberate North Korea
Soviet Union	• Achieved closer friendship with China • Conflict between China and America was to the Soviet Union's advantage	• Forced into expensive arms race with America
China	• Gained the respect of Asian Communists • Saved North Korea from America • Kept a crucial buffer state on the eastern frontier • Achieved closer friendship with the Soviet Union	• 900,000 casualties • Cost of the war • Failed to win South Korea for Communism • Increased American protection for Chiang Kaishek in Formosa • Isolated by America in trade and politics

The Korean War forced America into a new role in Asia. Through its policy of 'Containment' America became seen as the defender of democracy against the spread of Communism. America had no real wish to fight another Asian war, but what if other countries in the Far East fell to Communism? Would they not look to America?

America badly needed friends.

Along with NATO, America established its 'sphere of influence', surrounding the two Communist Great Powers. Predictably, the Soviet Union saw America's actions as further proof of 'encirclement'. It sought to strengthen its own 'sphere of influence' in its East European satellites, first through economics – 'Comecon' – and later through the 'Warsaw Pact' military alliance.

The Korean War was the first direct 'Hot' conflict between East and West within the Cold War. At one point, even nuclear weapons were considered as an option. Though the Korean War flashpoint passed, East–West tensions remained. America and the Soviet Union began an expensive and potentially deadly nuclear arms race.

Questions

1 Why did war break out in Korea? Use the table on page 26 to help you decide.

2 Write notes on each of the following:
a) Why America became involved in the Korean War;
b) Why the Soviet Union failed to stop UN forces going to Korea;
c) Why the UN (really America) tried to 'liberate' North Korea;
d) Why China sent 'volunteer' armies to Korea;
e) President Truman's wish to contain Communism.

3 Look at Source I. Do you think the US Secretary of State meant what he said? For what other reasons might he have made this speech?

4 Which of the three Great Powers gained, or lost, most from being involved in the Korean War (see table above)?

5 Two armed camps: 1945–60s

The nuclear arms race

▶ **What was the arms race?
How important was the arms race
as a factor in the Cold War?**

Doomsday

The atom bombs dropped on Hiroshima and
Nagasaki ended one war but helped to start
another.

The awful power of the atom bomb, shown in
Source **A**, brought Doomsday to Hiroshima at
8.16 am on 6 August 1945.

Source A A nuclear test explosion at Bikini Atoll, 1946

Out of a population of 255,000, 45,000 died
on that day, and over the next four months the
total rose to 64,000. It had a devastating effect
on the buildings.

Yet within a few years
bombs existed that were
2,500 times more powerful
than the Hiroshima atom
bomb!

Source B
Devastated Hiroshima

The nuclear card

The destructive power of
nuclear weapons became a
vital factor in relations
between the Great Powers
from 1945 onwards.

At first, America alone
held the scientific secrets
and technology to create the
atomic bomb. No matter
how many *conventional*
ground, sea or air forces the
Soviet Union had, America
was the world's most
powerful military country. As
the Cold War developed,
America wished to stay in
first place, ahead of the Soviet Union.

Stalin was determined that the Soviet Union
should become a Great Power with a nuclear
capability to compete with America. Despite the risks
and financial costs, both East and West set out on a
race to equip themselves with even more lethal
nuclear weapons.

The leaders of the Great Powers came to realise
that if the Cold War ever turned into 'hot war', the
use of nuclear weapons would result in tens of
millions of dead on either side, and the extinction of
mankind.

Why did both Great Powers allow the nuclear arms
race to *escalate*? Source **C** gives an American view of
the events up to 1960.

1945

America has the advantage over the Soviet Union. We are the only country with the nuclear secrets for making the bomb.

Stalin is frightened of the destructive power of the bomb. No doubt Soviet scientists will develop an atom bomb, but it might take them 20 years. In the meantime, America holds the trump card against any Soviet threat of 'hot war'. Our policy of *containment* means that we can station American bombers in countries in Western Europe. Our long-range bombers can fly 6,000 miles to strike at the Soviet Union if they have to.

September 1949

The Soviet Union have exploded an atomic bomb! We did not think they could become a nuclear power so soon. We must build up our stocks of nuclear weapons against this new threat. Our scientists tell us that a superbomb is possible – a hydrogen bomb with 2,500 times more explosive power than our first atom bombs.

1950

One of our nuclear scientists has been spying for the Soviets.

1952

Our first H-bomb (hydrogen bomb) test in the Pacific goes well. One H-bomb could destroy Moscow. We must concentrate on ringing the Soviet Union with bases in friendly countries. We must build more H-bombs and more bombers.

1953

The Soviet Union has exploded an H-bomb in Siberia. They are catching up with us in nuclear knowledge! And they have a new long-range bomber. American cities could be attacked. We still have many more nuclear bombs than the Soviet Union but must make many more and test new ones. We must *deter* the Soviet Union by fear of what we would do to their cities if they attacked us.

Bombers are slow – they could be shot down on the way to the target. The new H-bombs are smaller. Perhaps fighter aircraft could carry them? Or cannons … submarines … rockets?

The Soviet Union are testing even bigger H-bombs.

4 October 1957

The Soviet Union have launched a satellite, Sputnik 1, into space – before America. The Soviet Union is ahead in rocket development. The rocket that launched Sputnik 1 could be fitted with a nuclear warhead. The missiles could be fired from thousands of miles away. The Soviet Union are building thousands of these ICBMs (Inter-Continental Ballistic Missiles). Twenty million Americans would be wiped out in one day if the Soviet Union attacked. Twenty-two million would die later, from radiation. What are we to do? Our early warning system across the North Pole is no use any more.

The Soviet Union have many more missiles than America. Every year they show them off in Moscow. But would they use them? Our bombs can still destroy Russian cities. We must build up our missiles and bombs. Our ICBMs have a range of 5,000 miles at 16,000 miles per hour. Perhaps we should concentrate on short-range nuclear weapons? They could be used across the frontiers of Europe. If it comes to nuclear war with the Soviet Union, better to destroy Europe in a 'limited war' than America. Perhaps the Soviet Union will agree?

1958–61

The Soviet Union might have enough ICBNs to knock out America with one blow! We still need to be able to deter the Soviets by developing 'second strike' power – to attack the Soviet Union harder than they might attack us. We must protect our nuclear weapons from being hit by the Soviet Union's first strike. We need to develop warheads that can be fired from underground missile sites, or from mobile missile launchers.

July 1960

One of our submarines has fired a new missile – Polaris – from under the sea. Polaris missiles have a range of 1,500 miles. Now nowhere in the Soviet Union is safe from attack from undersea submarines. The Soviet Union are bound to strengthen their missile sites, and are developing missile-firing submarines. America may be in the lead in the nuclear arms race now, but we must stockpile more weapons in order to deter Soviet attack. We need more Polaris missiles and more ICBMs. We must make use of outer space for spy satellites. We must develop defensive anti-ballistic missiles which could destroy Soviet ICBMs before they reach their target … .

Question

Make up a time chart like that above with notes explaining how the Soviet Union might see these events in the arms race. Mention Hiroshima and Nagasaki (1945); American bases in NATO countries (after 1949); the American H-bomb (1952); the Russian H-bomb (1953); the threat to Russian cities; Sputnik 1; use of space; Britain's first H-bomb (1957); 'limited war' in Europe; Polaris submarines; American underground missile silos; America's stockpile of nuclear warheads.

Two armed camps 1949–55

▶ **How did Great Power conflict lead to a global re-grouping?**

Was the Soviet Union right to see the American bases as a threat? How had this situation arisen? Viewpoints (below) should help you remember.

Source A   Written by a Soviet student, 1958

The matter is very simple ... any Soviet citizen can explain it to you. The United States is surrounding us with bases which are ready to fire atomic bombs.

1953: what should Americans do?

Think about the events in Viewpoints (below) through American eyes. Which of these plans would you advise President Eisenhower to follow:
a)   Try to arrange a top-level meeting with Stalin to talk about ending the Cold War?
b)   Try to make treaties to surround the Soviet Union with countries friendly to America?
c)   Try to liberate the countries of Eastern Europe already under the Soviet Union?
d)   Increase America's military power by developing new weapons?

America's leaders decided on plans **b)** and **d)**. Between 1949 and 1955 a series of Treaties were signed between America and friendly non-Communist countries. Many of America's allies became sites for American missile and bomber bases.

1955: what should the Soviet Union do?

How would the Communist Great Powers view America's actions? Think about the situation through Soviet eyes. What would you advise the Soviet Union's new leaders to do?
a)   Increase spending on arms and develop new weapons to counter the American threat?
b)   Make moves to lower tension by talking to America's leaders?
c)   Look for friendship with Mao Zedong, in the hope of the Soviet Union and China becoming Communist allies?
d)   Bind the Communist countries of Eastern Europe to the Soviet Union in a military agreement.

The Soviet Union decided on plans **b)**, **c)** and **d)**.

So, the decade which began with the defeat of Hitler's Germany, ended with the world re-grouped into two armed camps. It became known as a *bipolar* world – with countries friendly to America in the West and the Soviet Union in the East (see Source **B**).

 Viewpoints

For each of the statements below ask yourself:
• Is it the view of America or the USSR?
• What event is being described?
• What is the correct order of the events?
(Clue – they all happened from 1946–53.)

1 a)   We must be strong to defend the West against Communism.
b)   NATO is proof of an American threat against us.

2 a)   At last we have a friend in China. But China is backward.
b)   Mao's victory in China is a big blow. We must protect non-Communist countries in the Far East.

3 a)   They are out to expand into Western Europe. We must prevent this.
b)   They have the bomb. We must have friendly countries in Eastern Europe.

4 a)   They have no right to attack North Korea.
b)   They are giving aid to North Korea. We must act.

Now draw up a table like this and fill in your ideas.

Source B   A bipolar world

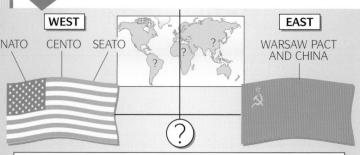

Many Third World countries in South America, Africa and Asia were 'non aligned': that is, not under direct influence from West or East

American view	Soviet view	Event	Year
1b	1a	'Iron Curtain' Speech	1946

Protect … survive … protest

▶ **What was the idea of deterrence?**
Why was it MAD?
How did governments and ordinary people react to the threat of nuclear war?

Protect

Each Great Power, fearful of the other, used every possible means to persuade its own civilians of the military need to protect themselves with vast stock piles of nuclear weapons.

Source A Extract from *When the Wind Blows*

MAD

By 1953 both Great Powers had new leaders. Would President Eisenhower and Premier Khruschev continue the arms race?

After Hiroshima both were aware that a full-scale nuclear war would result in total destruction. The idea of *deterrence* developed, which meant that if either side attacked, they could be sure of swift retaliation by the other. To deter one another both sides produced the capacity for 'overkill' and threatening 'Mutually Assured Destruction' on a global scale. Yet, despite the high risks, both America and the Soviet Union threatened to use the bomb during Cold War flashpoints.

What chance survival?

What might be the chances of surviving a nuclear holocaust? It depended upon who you were. For a tiny number of selected officials – political and military leaders – specially constructed and equipped nuclear bunkers were built below ground. But no official shelters were built for the millions of ordinary people. Some individuals built their own shelters. In Britain the government issued Civil Defence leaflets, which suggested helpful ways for civilians to protect themselves against nuclear attack. Source **A** shows how two cartoon characters react to receiving such advice about Civil Defence.

Protest

The Great Powers were similar in how little they allowed their own people to make organised protests. In America Cold War propaganda against the 'Red Menace' of Communism meant that – by and large – people supported their government. To protest was seen as 'un-American' or, worse still, 'pro-Communist'. Despite this, by the early 1960s groups of nuclear bomb protesters were active.

In Britain, also, a growing nuclear protest movement gathered strength. Members of the Campaign for Nuclear Disarmament participated in annual Easter marches.

In contrast, the rigid state control of citizens in the Soviet Union meant that no public protests were ever allowed.

***Q**uestion*

1 Since the Great Powers avoided nuclear war, does it mean that the ideas of deterrence, 'overkill' and MAD worked?

2 Look at Source **A**.
a) How do the man and woman see the situation? **b)** What does the author think about Civil Defence?

3 If there was no real defence against nuclear attack, why did the British government distribute 'Protect and Survive'?

Super Powers in space

▶ **Why did the Great Powers compete in a 'Space Race'?
How did events in the Space Race
affect the Cold War?**

Why did the Space Race begin?

By the mid-1950s, America and the Soviet Union
were locked in the icy grip of the Cold War. Yet,
despite having created the possibility of nuclear
doomsday, each still wished to prove themselves
as the most powerful.

What avenues remained open? The on-going
nuclear arms race offered the ideal chance. New
research was developed to launch rockets beyond
the atmosphere into outer space. To achieve this
would be an amazing achievement; worthy only of
a true Super Power.

Many key scientists' and technicians' work was
switched in a desperate attempt to be the 'first
into space'.

Both America and the Soviet Union began a
vastly expensive 'Space Race'; largely to prove to
the other that their own economic, technological
and political system was the most advanced.

Source A *Daily Express* headline announcing the flight of Sputnik

'Sputnik' to 'Sea of Tranquillity'

Sources **A** to **E** show some key events in the Great
Power Space Race. Initially, as Sources **A** and **B** show,
the Soviet Union's space programme gained major
successes, which won worldwide publicity. Equally
important was the impact on the American people. If
the Soviet Union had this level of
technology, then they could
really threaten America.

With America feeling
vulnerable, President
Kennedy threw down a new
challenge (Source **C**) to be
the first nation to land on
the moon. Both Great
Powers took up the
challenge. Sources **D** and **E**
reveal the outcome.

Source B
Yuri Gagarin in
Moscow.

> I believe that this nation should
> commit itself to achieving the
> goal, before this decade is out, of
> landing a man on the Moon and
> returning him safely to Earth.

Source C Photograph of
President Kennedy, plus extract
from a speech made by Kennedy
in May 1961

Source D Photograph of Neil Armstrong, plus his most famous words

I'm going to step off the ladder now. That's one small step for man, one giant leap for mankind.

Source E
Photograph of Buzz Aldrin on the Moon's surface. How was this picture taken?

Why did the Space Race end?

Many people thought that the Space Race was a costly, unproductive activity. Combined with the massive costs and key changes in Great Power relations, the Space Race came to an end.

More recent explorations of space have become one of the main areas of Great Power cooperation (see Source **A**, page 92).

Questions

1 Why did the Great Powers compete in the Space Race?

2 Watch the news and record any examples of Great Power cooperation in space.

6 Cold War: strategies and tactics

Love Story: Cold War style

▶ *What is your image of Great Power spying?*
How does your image of spying compare with the real life example?
What sort of tactics did spies use?

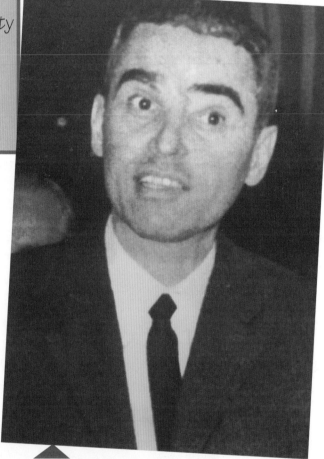

Source A Heinz Sutterlin

An unexpected caller

In 1959, Leonore Heinz was 31 and lonely. She lived in a large block of flats in Bonn, West Germany. By day she worked as a secretary in the Foreign Ministry of the West German Government.

One evening the doorbell rang. Outside, as Source **A** shows, stood a handsome man, clutching a bunch of red roses.

'Fraulein Newmann?' Leonore knew no one of that name.

'No, I'm sorry. Have you got the right address?' The man checked a piece of paper, apologised and turned to go. Then a thought struck him.

'Here, you have these for the trouble I've caused you.' Leonore was pleasantly surprised. She invited the man into her flat while she put the flowers in water. He introduced himself as Heinz Sutterlin, a freelance photographer. Over coffee they chatted and found they had many things in common. Heinz invited Leonore out to dinner a few nights later.

The months passed. Leonore saw more and more of Heinz. He showered her with dinner dates, gifts, concert tickets and visits. In December 1960 Heinz and Leonore were married. They decided that Leonore should keep up her job, since Heinz's income was unreliable.

Leonore's dilemma

One day Sutterlin asked Leonore to bring home some papers from her work. She was shocked and refused.

Heinz insisted. What was Leonore to do? She was torn between her feelings of guilt, her love for Heinz and her fear of losing him. At last she gave in.

Each lunchtime Leonore brought home papers in her handbag. While she cooked lunch, Heinz photographed the documents. In the afternoon Leonore returned them. No one ever knew. In five years Sutterlin passed 3,000 Foreign Ministry documents – a third of them secret – to his *contact* or case officer, a man called Runge.

Runge was an *agent* for the Soviet spying organisation, the KGB, which was based in Moscow. He had worked *undercover* in West Germany for many years.

Betrayed

All went well for Heinz and Leonore until 1967. Then secretly Runge switched sides. He became a *double agent* for the West. He gave the names of all his agents in West Germany to America's spying organisation, the *CIA* (Central Intelligence Agency). Heinz and Leonore were arrested by the West German authorities and put on trial for spying.

At the trial it became clear that Sutterlin had trained as a spy for the East German Ministry of State Security. In 1959 he was *taken over* by Runge, who ordered him to marry a secretary from the West German Foreign Ministry.

Leonore was heartbroken when she realised that their romance and marriage had all been part of a Soviet KGB plan. Three weeks later, unable to live with the truth, Leonore committed suicide in her cell. She hanged herself with her nightdress.

The wider picture

Leonore Sutterlin was just one victim of the shadowy, undercover world of spying. The importance of the Sutterlins' work to the KGB was made clear by Runge (see Source **B**).

Source B
Comment made by KGB agent Runge

> We read official reports from abroad, even before the West German Foreign Minister.

The Sutterlin story showed up the three main features of Great Power spying operations. First, *gathering information* from a potential enemy. For the most part, the collection of KGB intelligence data from the West German Foreign Ministry was a routine matter. Once obtained by Leonore (the *sub-agent*) and Heinz (the *principal agent*), the information was passed on by Runge to his superiors. Finally, it was studied by KGB officers who were experts in West German affairs.

The second feature is that of *counter-intelligence*. Both the CIA and the KGB tried to protect the secrecy of their agents and the work they are doing. Sometimes *false information* is deliberately *leaked* to confuse the opposition. Each side went to great lengths to gain information about the other's intelligence activities. In the case of the Sutterlins, the CIA were only able to find out what they were doing when the KGB agent, Runge, changed sides.

The Sutterlin story also includes the third feature of Great Power spying. That is *covert operations* – interfering in the politics of other countries. The American and Soviet governments used their intelligence agencies to support the governments of friendly countries and to put pressure on unfriendly ones. Cash aid, arms supplies, propaganda and spy training are some of the common forms of support or pressure.

Questions

1 a) Why was Leonore chosen?
b) What does her selection show about Great Power motives at that time?
c) What false identity did Heinz use?
d) How did Heinz become a spy?
e) Was Leonore forced to turn into a spy?
f) How long did Heinz and Leonore operate for?
g) What sort of information do you think Leonore may have passed on to Heinz?
h) What role did Runge play:
   i) at the start?
   ii) in the middle?
   iii) at the end?

2 Leonore's story reveals many features of Cold War spying. Re-read the story, then match spying terms to each of the three main characters. Use the Venn diagram as shown:

- East German
- West German
- KGB

- CIA
- double agent
- undercover
- take-over
- intelligence documents
- intelligence
- covert operations
- Soviet Union
- America
- counter intelligence

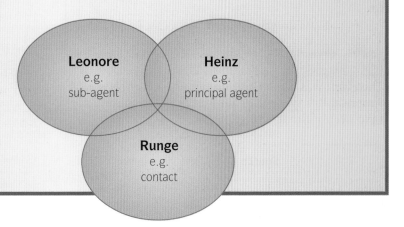

Leonore e.g. sub-agent

Heinz e.g. principal agent

Runge e.g. contact

Propaganda

> How did America and the Soviet Union use propaganda within their own countries and against each other?
> How did each Great Power use propaganda to put pressure on their citizens?

The war of words

Throughout the Cold War both sides made great use of propaganda. The war of words became an important weapon. Each Great Power used propaganda to support its own political system and to attack that of the other. The capitalist West attacked Communism. The Communist East attacked capitalism. Every form of mass-media – radio, books, newspapers, posters, film and speeches – has been used. As the Cold War deepened both Great Powers found ways to pressure its own people to conform. Here again, propaganda played its part. Finally, both Great Powers used propaganda to present their version of the truth.

'The American way'

By 1949 America had the highest standard of living in the world. Millions were taught to take pride in the best country in the world. Everyday all its school children swore the 'Oath of Allegiance'.

Communism with its alternative ideas, newly created atomic weapons and Chinese millions, was seen as a threat to the American way of life. Source **A** is a cartoon which suggests how the Soviet Union's motives were seen.

Have you ever taken part in a 'Living History' style event? To show what could lie ahead, one small town in America acted out a Soviet 'take-over' for a day. Source **B** recalls the local newspaper headlines:

Source A American cartoon showing the Soviet Union's hostile motives

MOSINEE SEIZED BY REDS!

COMMUNIST COUP IN WISCONSIN

Source B
Newspaper
headlines

The event was filmed and shown as a newsreel across America. Bill Sweinler organised the 'Communist' take-over of the school.

Source C Bill Sweinler remembering the take-over

The Americanism programme was developed to teach pride in bring an American. Because of this day we had, the kids who went to school saw first-hand that we'd got it pretty good as Americans'.

From *The People's Century*, BBC, 1997

Through careful propaganda, such as Source **D**, Stalin created a public image of himself as the 'Great Leader'.

To celebrate Stalin's 70th birthday, vast celebrations were held. Tamara Bauketik, then aged 11, offered a speech (see Source **D**). Yet, many years later her memories reveal the aura of Stalin's power (Source **E**).

Images of the enemy

The Soviet Union could not match America's standard of living. Yet, here again, propaganda played its part in creating a public image of America.

> Lies (and distortions) ... fill the American ... (reactionary) press. What is their culture like? A millionaire's dog is a luxury. The unemployed queue for food.

In contrast, through propaganda, the Soviet Union's citizens – like Tamara Bauketik in Source **G** – believed differently.

Source G Tamara Bauketik

> We knew our society was just and that capitalism was terrible and that people were exploited. That's what we were taught. It didn't matter how badly I lived now. I hoped it would get better. I believed in Stalin and knew it would improve.
>
> From *The People's Century*, BBC, 1997

America's actions were shown to be hostile, by encircling the Soviet Union, as Source **H** shows.

> We are children of Lenin and Stalin. We strive to the summit of learning: teacher, leader, beloved friend. Father Stalin, welcome!

Source D Greeting to Stalin, upon his 70th birthday

> I was transported into a fairytale. I had eyes only for him. He had such kindly eyes. It was as if he were my father. I just wanted to touch him.
>
> From *The People's Century*, BBC, 1997

Source E Tamara Bauketik recalls Stalin's impact upon her

Source F Extract from Soviet cinema newsreel

Source H Cartoon showing America attempting to encircle the Soviet Union

1 Draw up a chart to show the range of propaganda from Source **A** to Source **H**, e.g.

Source letter	Type of Source	American or Soviet	Key message

2 Which of the two cartoons (Sources **A** or **H**) do you find most effective and why?

3 Which key point about Great Power motives are the cartoons trying to make?

4 What is the value of cartoon evidence given that it is simply propaganda?

5 Consider Tamara Kauketik's evidence in Sources **D**, **E** and **G**.
  a) How far did she seem to believe Stalin's propaganda about:
    i) himself
    ii) America
    iii) the future of the Soviet Union.
  b) Does the fact that Tamara's attitudes were based upon propaganda – rather than truth – make them unreliable to a student of the Cold War?

Questions

Shifts in tactics

▶ *How did the Great Powers use propaganda to pressure their own citizens into accepting their ideology?*
How did Stalin's death lead to a 'thaw' in Great Power relations?

The thaw: radio-waves

Technology such as that in Source **A** allowed Cold War propaganda to be sent across artificial boundaries, such as the Iron Curtain.

Alexei Kozlov a Moscow student recalls, in Source **B**, how important such broadcasts were.

Source A A radio transmitter mast

Source B Alexei Kozlov

The Radio was our only access. The West and neighbours could denounce you for listening to those stations. Jazz was banned. They put out propaganda about Americans … there was a saying 'Today he plays jazz and tomorrow he betrays the nation.

From *The People's Century*, BBC, 1997

This station, daily, pierces the Iron Curtain with the truth, answering the lies of the Kremlin and bringing a message of hope to millions trapped behind the Iron Curtain. The 'Crusade for Freedom' is your chance, and mine, to fight Communism.

Radio broadcasts were seen as an opportunity by America. Western propaganda was spread from stations like the 'Voice of America' through transmitters in West Germany. One broadcaster, later to become well-known as America's President (1980–88: see page 68) was Ronald Reagan.

Source C Ronald Reagan's 'Airwaves' appeal, cinema newsreel, *c*.1950s

Fears and reactions

Both Great Powers became frightened. What if the rival ideology spread inside their own countries? This fear led, in turn, to official investigations into thousands of people suspected of holding rival sympathies or beliefs.

In America, anti-Communist scares grew. Between 1946 and 1954, a series of 'Witch Hunts' took place against Americans suspected of being Communists. Senator Joseph McCarthy became feared in his prosecutions against claims of 'Reds Under Beds'. After public questioning, those found 'guilty' might lose their jobs, income, status and friends – but no more.

In contrast, in Stalin's era anyone found 'guilty' of similar anti-State activities, such as Alexei Kozlov in Source **B**, might be imprisoned'. Worse still, they might join the millions sent to serve long sentences in forced labour camps where only a few survived. These millions simply disappeared without trace.

Other officials, often important Party members in Eastern bloc countries, were brought to high-profile 'Show Trials' filmed and shown to Soviet citizens.

Thousands were executed. Through a mixture of rigid state control, backed by a vast security system, Stalin ruled the Soviet Union: a public hero, but a private monster.

Stalin dies

In 1953 Stalin died. In Russia, and in the Communist countries of Eastern Europe, millions heaved a sigh of relief. Now people began to ask who would follow Stalin. What would be his attitude to the satellites of Eastern Europe? To America? To Communist China? How would US President Eisenhower react? After all, the Americans saw Stalin as a main reason for the development of the Cold War (see Source **D**).

The thaw

By 1953 the Cold War rules had changed. Each side could now destroy the other with H-bombs. Was this a chance for a thaw in the icy temperature of the Cold War? President Eisenhower hoped so (see Source **E**).

For two years the Soviet Union seemed to have several leaders. In 1955 Nikita Khruschev emerged as a clear leader. Khruschev was totally unlike the sinister Stalin. He loved to travel, and show off Soviet achievements. His personality seemed to offer a chance for better East–West relations. How was such an improvement to come about? Winston Churchill, Britain's Prime Minister, thought a conference at the highest level (a *summit*) should take place between the leading powers.

Kruschev liked the idea of a Summit Conference between the leaders of America, China, Britain, France and the Soviet Union. A meeting was arranged for July 1955 in Geneva, Switzerland. Hopes ran high in Europe. In fact little was agreed at Geneva, but at least the Great Powers met on friendly terms. The Soviets said later 'it was a turning point in the relations between the Soviet Union and the West'.

'Peaceful co-existence'

A year later, in 1956, Khruschev told a meeting of top Communists that Stalin had been a bad and cruel leader. In a key phrase he also commented on the Soviet Union's dealings with the rest of the world:

There are only two ways: either peaceful co-existence, or the most destructive war in history. There is no third way.

Source F   Extracts from Premier Khrushev's speech, 1956

Behind Khruschev's idea of *peaceful co-existence* lay the basic idea that war between East and West did not have to happen.

Containment – America should encircle the Soviet Union with countries friendly to America.

Massive retaliation – the Korean War taught America that next time she should fight Communism with a massive nuclear attack on the Soviet Union.

Roll back – America should help the peoples of Eastern Europe, if they revolted against the control of the Soviet Communists.

Source D   Dulles' ideas

The new Soviet leadership has a precious opportunity to help turn the tide of history ... we welcome every act of peace.

Source E   President Eisenhower, April 1953

Khruschev was telling his audience three things: that in the age of H-bombs the ideas of Marx and Lenin were out-of-date and dangerous; that the Soviet Union should live peaceably with America, even if the two powers did not like one another; that the Soviet Union should work for Communist revolutions in other countries through peaceful means.

For the Soviet satellite countries of Eastern Europe 'peaceful coexistence' looked promising. Under Stalin's rule they had been tied to Moscow. Now Khruschev's ideas suggested that the Soviet view of Communism was not the only path the satellites could take. Khruschev himself had spoken of 'different roads to Socialism'. Was Moscow's vice-like grip on the satellites over? Millions of Poles, Czechs and Hungarians hoped so.

Questions

1 Why was the radio so useful for propaganda (see Sources **A** and **B**?

2 What caused each Great Power to investigate its own citizens beliefs?

3 List the key events which combined to create 'the thaw' in the Great Power conflict.

4 **a)** Explain in your own words what Kruschev meant by 'peaceful co-existence'.
b) How did he think this shift in tactics would help the Communist cause in the Soviet Union and the rest of the world?

5 Why did Khruschev's ideas give hope to many Eastern Europeans?

Sex and spies, secrets and summits

▶ **What sort of people became spies?**
What were the Profumo and U2 affairs?
What were their effects on East–West relations?

Despite the 'thaw' both Great Powers continued to spy on each other.

Winston Churchill described the world of spying as the 'Battle of the Conjurors' – a war between experts in deception. From the start of the Cold War there was a massive growth in spying operations. It became vital for each side to know what the other was doing, or thinking of doing.

Myth and reality

The 'James Bond' image of the spy is a myth. The reality of spying is simply routine and distinctly unglamorous. What sort of people were willing to betray national secrets? Stories of spies affected every country. These key incidents, concerning Britain, reveal many elements.

In Britain the oldest universities like Oxford and Cambridge acted as fertile recruiting grounds. Some students supported Communist ideas. In later life many men from these universities rose to positions of power in political life, the Civil Service, the Armed Forces and business activities.

After a time, some spies such as diplomats Kim Philby and Guy Burgess – defected to the Soviet Union. Others, like Sir Anthony Blunt, worked in the Civil Service for many years, whilst spying undercover, until his detection.

Sex and spying

Sex was used as a means of obtaining secrets.

In Spring 1963 Britain was rocked by the 'Profumo Scandal'. At its centre was Christine Keeler, a high-class call girl.

John Profumo, a Government Minister, was accused – amidst high publicity – of an extra marital liaison with her. Amongst Keeler's other 'clients' was a Soviet naval attache. After widespread public concern, Profumo was forced to resign in disgrace.

Elsewhere, many KGB agents obtained Western secrets through using the 'Honey Trap'. Beautiful young Soviet girls would be used as bait to catch unsuspecting businessmen and, after illicit sex, demands to reveal intelligence secrets would be made, or if not, then blackmail threats would follow.

> ### Superpower spying organisations
>
> **America** The *CIA* was set up by President Truman in 1947 to 'perform … functions and duties relating to intelligence affecting the national security.' Today the CIA has over 12,000 intelligence officers with about 4,000 agents active in foreign countries.
>
> **Russia** The *KGB* came into being after Stalin's death in 1953. It developed from Stalin's feared secret police. At its height the KGB employed 25,000 people on gathering intelligence from foreign countries. It operated between 3,000 and 5,000 agents in over 90 different countries.

Markus Wolff, former head of the East German Secret Service, the Stasi, scooped up most of West Germany's secrets by employing a legion of handsome, virile officers to seduce a generation of middle-aged women civil servants who had been deprived of sex and romance because most of the eligible West German men had been killed in the war.

Source A The *Independent on Sunday*, 1 June 1997. Can you recall the names of two victims of Wolff's methods?

A spy and a summit

January 1960. As the new decade dawned, hopes of real progress in relations between America and the Soviet Union seemed possible. Yet, one incident was about to set this back.

The U2 affair

1 Peshawar, Pakistan, 1 May 1960. An American pilot, Gary Powers, takes off from his base. He is flying a Lockheed U2. It is a long-range, high-altitude spy plane. Powers' mission is to take photographs of military sites in the Soviet Union before landing at a NATO base in Norway. He is working for the CIA. The U2 is armed and the flight is dangerous. But America has been flying such missions for four years. Each one has been a success.

2 The flight goes well; the U2 photographs sites deep in the Soviet Union. Then disaster strikes. Flying at 68,000 feet above the Ural Mountains the aircraft is suddenly hit. Powers loses control as the U2 dives earthwards. He ejects from the aircraft and

parachutes to the ground. The U2 crashes near Sverdlovsk. Four days later Premier Khruschev announces the news that an American plane has been shot down over the Soviet Union. No details are given. What was America to think? What should they say?

3 On 7 May NASA announced that a U2 research plane used 'to study weather conditions at high altitude' had been missing since 1 May when its pilot 'reported that he was having oxygen difficulties over Lake Van, Turkey area'. The same day the American Government said, 'there was no deliberate attempt to violate (fly into) Soviet air space and never has been'.

4 America denied that spy flights over the Soviet Union happened. America asked the Soviet Union for more information. On 7 May Khruschev announced the full facts. The U2 had been shot down by a Soviet missile. Gary Powers had been captured 'alive and well'. He had admitted that he was on a spying mission. On his person were a poison pen and a silent pistol. Film taken on the U2's flight had been developed showing Soviet military sites.

The Soviet Union had concrete proof. Not only had America been caught spying, but the American Government had also lied about the U2 flight. America had to admit to a spying operation
    Khruschev demanded a full apology from America.

The Paris summit

The future of the Paris summit talks, only days away, lay on a knife edge, as Source **C** shows.

    Khruschev was still prepared for the summit meeting to go ahead, providing Eisenhower admitted that the CIA made the U2 flights without his permission. This he would not do. Eisenhower said the flights were 'a vital necessity'.

    As the leaders made their way to Paris, the U2 incident was still hot news. One day before the summit Khruschev listed his demands to America:
- America must apologise for the U2 affair.
- America must stop flights in the future.
- America must punish those responsible.
    Eisenhower refused to apologise. The Paris Summit ended in uproar. Khruschev stormed out in anger and returned to Moscow. The U2 incident made Eisenhower very unpopular. Khruschev cancelled an invitation for Eisenhower to visit the Soviet Union. The Soviet Union condemned America's action at the United Nations.

    Gary Powers was put on trial in Moscow and sentenced to 10 years imprisonment. (He was released in 1962 in exchange for a Soviet master spy.)

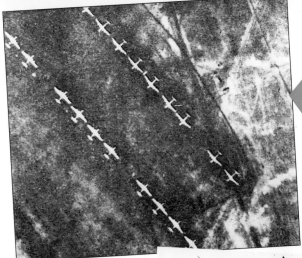

Source B
Russian military airfield, allegedly photographed by Gary Powers

Source C
How would the U2 affair affect the Paris Summit?

American forces went on worldwide alert straight after the summit.

    Many people felt that America had ruined progress in East–West relations, and had threatened world peace.

    Communist China thought that the U2 incident confirmed its view that Khruschev's idea of peaceful co-existence with America was wrong. America could never be trusted.

    The 'thaw' was over. The icy chill of the Cold War days returned to relations between America and the Soviet Union.

Questions

1 Why was sex a powerful weapon in the world of spying?

2 Why was the U2 incident so damaging to America?

3 **a)** What point is Source **C** making?
    b) What symbol of peace is shown in the cartoon?
    c) Do you think this is a Western or a Communist view of the U2 incident. Why?

4 Explain what effect the U2 incident had on relations between the Great Powers in 1960 (America/the Soviet Union; the Soviet Union/China; China/America).

5 Why did the U2 incident lead to the end of the 'thaw'?

7 Great Power flashpoints: 1956–68

Satellite revolts: Hungary

What caused Hungary to revolt against Soviet control in 1956?
What was the Soviet Union's reaction to the events? Why did they react as they did?

Stalin's satellites

Stalin had treated East Germany, Poland and Hungary almost as 'slave colonies' of the Soviet Union. Hungary had to pay war reparations in food and goods to the Soviet Union. The standard of living in Eastern Europe got steadily worse; shortages of food were common. Workers in farms and factories were told to work harder for less. Each satellite had a feared secret police, prisons and labour camps. In Hungary alone 25,000 people had been executed without trial since 1945. Stalin-style Communism in Eastern Europe had left the people downtrodden and angry. In 1955 the satellites had been forced to sign the Warsaw Pact, binding their military fate to the Soviet Union still further.

Peaceful co-existence?

In 1956 Premier Khruschev's speech attacking Stalin's leadership sent shock waves through Russian satellites in Eastern Europe.

Now, with Khruschev's speech, people in the satellite countries saw new hope. They wanted three things:
- a higher standard of living;
- less direction from the Soviet Union in economic life
- more political freedom from the Soviet Union.

Each satellite wanted to develop a Communist society in its own way.

How would the Soviet Union react to these ideas? Although, Kruschev had begun the process of *De-Stalinisation*, would the Soviet Union really allow her satellites to make changes? How would the West react if any changes were allowed?

Unrest began in Poland. In July 1956 a revolt against harsh living and working conditions broke out. Khruschev flew to Poland and told the people his feelings (see Source **A**).

> We have shed our blood to liberate this country and now you want to hand it over to the Americans.

Source A Khruschev's pronouncement to the Polish people

The revolt was settled by Russia granting the Poles some reforms.

The revolt begins

News of the Polish revolt spread to Budapest in Hungary. Source **B** shows what happened there.

Source B During the revolt in Budapest a huge statue of Stalin was toppled to the ground and later dragged through the streets by a dustcart

George Mikes was one Hungarian rebel who provided an eye witness acount of this event (see Source **C**).

Source C George Mikes, Budapest, 1956

> Tempers were running high. A few thousand people went to the city park and surrounded the gigantic statue of Stalin. They got a rope round the neck and began to pull it ... then it toppled slowly forward – laughter and applause greeted the symbolic fall of the former tyrant.
>
> From *The People's Century*, BBC, 1996

As the protest gathered strength, protesters and security police clashed at a radio station. Soviet tanks rolled into the city. A battle developed, again witnessed by George Mikes.

Street fighting raged on for five days. The Hungarian rebels were backed by the Hungarian Army. Only the Security Police stayed loyal to the Soviet Union. Hundreds of police were lynched by the rebels.

The Soviet Unionists were not strong enough to crush the revolt. After talks with Imran Nagy, the new Hungarian Prime Minister, the Soviet tanks pulled out of Budapest. The rebels went wild with delight.

Reactions to the revolt

Was the Soviet Union going to allow a satellite to defeat the mighty Red Army? As news of the revolt came out of Hungary, how would the West react?

In America, President Eisenhower said: 'I feel with the Hungarian people.' Secretary of State, John Foster Dulles, congratulated the Hungarians for challenging the Red Army. Earlier, Dulles had spoken of 'rolling back' Communism in Eastern Europe (see Source **D**).

American radio stations in West Germany broadcast propaganda in support of the Hungarians. Many Hungarians believed that America would help them in their struggle against Moscow. But was America willing to run the risk of war to help the Hungarians?

On 1 November 1956, the Hungarians demanded far-reaching reforms. They wanted an end to the one-party system, and free elections. Hungary would withdraw from the Warsaw Pact and become a neutral, independent country.

A satellite is squashed

This was too much for the Soviet Union. They were afraid the iron curtain would be torn. Free elections could mean the end of Communism in Hungary. Other satellites might follow suit – that would lead to the end of the Soviet Union precious 'buffer zone' against the West.

Khruschev sought advice on what to do from the Chinese Communists. His decision was made easier by world events. America was facing a presidential election. America was angry with Britain and France over their recent invasion of Egypt. World attention had moved to the Middle East and away from Eastern Europe.

On 4 November 1956, 1,000 Russian tanks rumbled into Hungary. Bitter street fighting followed. Desperate radio appeals were broadcast. No aid came, only sympathy. Thirty thousand Hungarians were killed. Two hundred thousand fled to the West through Austria. Nagy was imprisoned and later

To all those suffering under Communist slavery, let us say: you can count on us.

Source D John Foster Dulles describes his 'Roll Back' theory

Source E Soviet tanks after rioting in Budapest

Source F George Mikes reported from the scene

We have almost no weapons. People are running up to the tanks, throwing in hand-grenades and closing the windows. The Hungarian people are not afraid of death. We have just heard a rumour that American troops will get here within an hour or two.

From *The People's Century*, BBC, 1996

executed. A new Soviet-backed government was installed.

By 14 November the fighting was over. The American *Time Magazine* reported on the outcome (see Source **G**).

Source G *Time Magazine*, November 1956

The steel-shod Soviet jackboot heeled down on Hungary this week, stamping and grinding out the young democracy.

Questions

1 Why did Hungary revolt against the Soviet Union in October 1956?

2 **Either**
   a) Imagine you are a Hungarian rebel taking part in the scenes in Sources **B** and **C, or**
   b) Imagine you are a Soviet tank commander during Sources **E** and **F**.
   Write about what you heard, saw and felt: during the events; an hour after the events took place.

3 'In his attempts at reform Khruschev released forces beyond his control and one of his satellites almost broke away' (*The Cold War*, Hastings)
   Explain why the Soviet Union was so worried about 'giving in' to Hungary.

Crisis in Berlin: the Wall

▶ **Why was the Berlin Wall built?**
How did Berliners react to the wall?
How did the West react to the Wall?

Source A West Berlin in the early 1960s, showing 'prosperity'

Background

At the centre of 'the German problem' lay Berlin. For 10 years after the Berlin airlift (see page 20) the city returned to 'normal life'. 'Normal' that is, for Berlin. It stayed a divided city – in a divided nation. Berliners crossed sector boundaries for work and pleasure. Some, called *defectors*, crossed from East to West, never to return. The city created a gaping hole in the Communist iron curtain.

Tension increases

In 1958 Kruschev tried to create a crisis over Berlin. He threatened to hand over the agreed Western access routes into West Berlin to East Germany, and told the occupying armies to withdraw from patrolling Berlin. This led to a war of nerves between East and West. In the end, Khruschev backed down, but the Berliners stayed tense. Defections increased to 20,000 a month, which created a serious shortage of workers in East Berlin.

Source B East Berlin in the early 1960s, showing 'drabness'

A city of contrasts

As Sources **A** and **B** show, West and East Berlin were quite different. West Berlin recovered quickly from the Second World War. Thanks to American and West German aid, West Berlin throbbed with life. Its department stores bulged with consumer goods. In contrast the streets and shops of East Berlin were drab; consumer goods were difficult to buy.

This contrast was clear to Otto Seidel. He lived in East Germany but visited relatives in West Germany. Otto was a skilled engineer. At work he was fed-up with the ever-higher work targets. At home, supplies of meat and vegetables were in short supply. In May 1961, Otto and his family defected to a refugee centre in West Berlin. All told, over two million East Germans did the same.

Kruschev acts

The *exodus* (mass escape) was a serious and embarrassing problem. East Germany and the Soviet Union had to do something. The hole in the iron curtain had to be filled. On 3 August the Soviet Government voiced its fears (see Source **C**).

> Before everyone's eyes West Germany is becoming a seat of war danger in Europe. An army headed by former Hitler generals has sprung up there. Today West Germany has the largest army on the European continent among the NATO member countries.

Source C Propaganda from the Soviet Government

The East German Government, under Soviet direction, acted.

13 August 1961

Police Sergeant Hans Peters and Ursula Heinemann were eye-witnesses to the events of 13 August 1961 in Berlin.

Hans was on border duty in the French Sector of West Berlin. At 2.20 am six trucks roared towards him, headlights blazing. Eighty yards away they stopped. A moment later the street was full of armed soldiers who set up machine guns aimed at the French Sector. Two guards approached carrying coils of barbed wire. At the invisible border line between the Soviet and French sectors the squads cordoned off the street. In the houses no one stirred.

At 4.45 am Ursula Heinemann awoke in her East Berlin flat to another working day at the Plaza Hotel in West Berlin. She walked to the nearby station and went to the ticket counter. 'Nein! Nein! Take your pfennigs back! It's all over now with trips to Berlin.'

At that moment Ursula saw five armed East German transport police heading her way. She turned and ran back to her flat. 'They've closed the border!' In a moment the landing and corridors of the flats were full of people shouting and crying.

She decided that she must cross to the West. But how? Near the US Sector she slipped through an orchard and reached the barbed wire border. Ursula crawled forward on her stomach. She felt the metal barbs tearing her skin. At last she reached a border post. A moment later, she was in West Berlin.

By early morning East German police and soldiers had cut the city in two. The seal-off operation went on. Only a few crossing points stayed open, protected by tanks, armoured cars and water cannons.

Nevertheless, some were still determined to risk death by crossing from East to West.

America's reaction

What would the West do? Worried West Berliners looked to America. America's new President, John F. Kennedy, wanted to show them support. Vice-President Johnson flew to Berlin. America protested to the Soviet Union about their action – but did no more. Kennedy was not willing to risk war over Berlin.

Wire becomes wall

On 17 August the barbed wire began to be replaced with stone. The Berlin Wall had begun. Where houses formed the border, their windows were bricked up. Once the wall was finished, the East–West border was sealed.

The effects of the Wall

The Wall was an ugly scar across Berlin. It became the most famous symbol of the Cold War (see Source **E**).

Source E   The Berlin Wall

The wall succeeded in stopping the flood of defectors to the West. Forty-one Germans were killed crossing the wall in its first year. Others, determined to defect, tunnelled their way to the West, under the Wall. Many families and friends were forced to live apart.

As for the Great Powers, it made both of them look weak. America failed to stop East Germany imprisoning its own people. Kruschev's efforts to force the West out of Berlin had also failed.

Questions

1 Why did the West give West Berlin massive aid after the Second World War?

2 Compare Sources **A** and **B**.
List the differences you can see in each source. In what way was a rich West Berlin a good advertisement for capitalism?

3 Describe how the Seidel family might feel:
   a) 6 months before their defection;
   b) on the night of their defection;
   c) on the day after their defection;
   d) on the day after the Berlin Wall was built.

4 Consider Khruschev's position (Source **C**). Was he justified in his decision to build the Berlin Wall?

Kennedy and the Cuban Missile Crisis

▶ *What caused the Cuban Missile Crisis to develop?*
Which leader, Kennedy or Khruschev, handled the crisis with most skill?
How close did the Great Powers come to nuclear war?

To the brink

What is your earliest memory of a major world event? How old were you?

Source A Memories of Peter Fisher, 1997

The very first world event I was ever aware of was when I was 10. I remember coming home from school and watching the tea-time news on our black and white TV. Each day it kept showing photos of ships. I didn't really follow what it was about. But I remember my uncle and mother going very quiet.

I was not alone. Other school children in Britain and America were aware of the adults' feelings of fear.

What train of events had brought the Great Powers to the edge of a nuclear war?

Source B shows a map with: American base, USA, Cape Canaveral, ATLANTIC OCEAN, N, Tampa, Key West, Gulf of Mexico, Havana, CUBA, Bay of Pigs, Guantánamo, HAITI, JAMAICA, Caribbean Sea, MEXICO, 0 km 500

Source B
Kennedy and the Cuban Missile Crisis

Cuba: fact file

At the centre of the crisis was the Caribbean island of Cuba, which is located only 90 miles south from mainland America (see Source **B**).

Before 1959

- Pro-American leaders.
- Many businesses owned by Americans.
- Most Cuban trade to America.
- Sugar, main crops, bought by America.
- Wide gulf between rich and poor.
- American military bases on Cuba.

After 1959

- Revolution: Fidel Castro takes over.
- Castro 'Anti-American' in ideas and actions.
- America refuse to buy sugar.
- Americans fail in attempts to invade Cuba and assassinate Castro.
- Castro turns to Soviet Union for help.
- Soviet Union agree to assist Cuba.
- Castro allows Soviet Union to set up nuclear missile bases in Cuba.

Two leaders

By the time of the crisis over Cuba, America had a new young President. John Kennedy, aged 43, was determined to appear 'strong'. Recently, his image had been tarnished. He failed to stop Kruschev's actions in Berlin (page 47). He failed to remove Castro from power in the 'Bay of Pigs' invasion.

Khruschev, aged 67, thought he could exploit Kennedy's youth and inexperience as a world leader to the Soviet Union's advantage.

The Soviet Union's new friendship with Cuba seemed an ideal invitation to establish military bases close to America. This would pressure America and test out Kennedy.

The crisis starts

In August 1962, 30 Soviet ships with mysterious cargoes, arrived in Cuba. Later, Soviet technicians followed.

In September 1962, America became worried about military bases on Cuba, its near neighbour. President Kennedy had warned Premier Khruschev not to put Soviet nuclear missiles on Cuba. Khruschev said he had no intention of doing so. What was going on? America had to find out.

U2 spy planes flew over Cuba and the Atlantic. Source **C** shows one of a series of photographs.

The CIA judge that these sites under construction are for Soviet nuclear missiles. Source **D** reveals their frightening calculations.

Robert Kennedy, the President's brother, wrote a blow-by-blow account of the crisis (see Source **E**).

Source C U2 photograph of missile sites being built on Cuba

Source D American towns within range of missiles from Cuba

Tuesday 16 October, 1962 President Kennedy asked me to come to the White House ... U2 reconnaissance had convinced (the CIA) that Russia was placing missiles and atomic weapons on Cuba.

Source E Extract from Robert Kennedy's memoirs of the Cuban crisis

○	Cities not within reach of missiles
◑	Cities within reach of short-range missiles
●	Cities within reach of medium-range missiles
▲	Missile sites
– – –	3200 kilometre range
······	1600 kilometre range

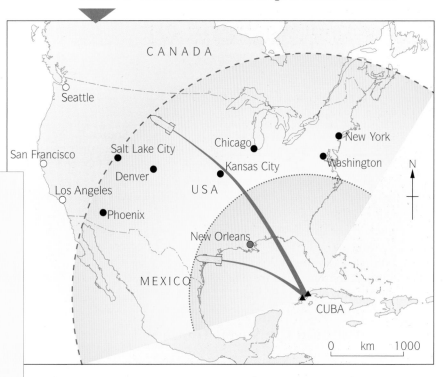

Here was proof that the Russians had been lying! Some missiles were on Cuba. Others were on Russian ships in the mid-Atlantic, heading for Cuba. America had to act.

So began the most serious crisis of the Cold War. It brought the USA and the Soviet Union to the brink of nuclear war and humanity to the edge of extinction. Two men, President Kennedy and Premier Khruschev, would decide the fate of the human race.

What should America do?

What was America's first step to be? The table below shows five possible options.

Cuban missile crises: options and considerations

Option	Advantages	Disadvantages
A Do nothing - allow missiles to be based in Cuba.	• Gives time to prepare response.	• Unpopular in America. Kennedy looks weak. • Major success to the Soviet Union. • Khruschev looks strong. • Threat to US security.
B Attack Cuba with nuclear weapons.	• Strike first – before the Soviet Union attacks America in same way.	• Full-scale nuclear war, millions killed – the end of humanity?
C Air strike against the Cuban missile bases, using non-nuclear weapons.	• Destroy missiles and sites already in Cuba.	• War with Cuba and perhaps the Soviet Union. • No guarantee all sites would be destroyed. • US casualties.
D Blockade Cuba with US Navy – no Russian ships allowed through.	• Limited pressure – could be increased later. • The Soviet Union would be forced to fire first shot to break blockade.	• Missiles and sites in Cuba would not be affected. • Conflict with the Soviet Union rather than Cuba. • The Soviet Union might do the same to West Berlin.
E Invasion of Cuba by US Armed Forces.	• Destroy missiles and sites.	• Previous attempt (1961) failed. • War with Cuba and perhaps the Soviets. • US casualties (estimated 25,000). • Soviets might invade West Berlin.

On 22 October, President Kennedy announced his decision (see Source **F**).

The blockade began on 24 October. Cuba was ringed by 100 American warships. America made other military moves. Plans for an invasion of Cuba were drawn up. Fifty-two bombers, armed with nuclear bombs, flew patrols. Rules for stopping and boarding the Russian ships were agreed between politicians and America's naval forces. America got support for its action from allies in South America and Europe.

What should the Soviet Union do?

How would the Russians react to America's 'blockade'. Would Americans really stop Russian ships or was America bluffing? The Soviet ships sailed on, escorted by a Russian submarine.

Was this the time to pressure Kennedy through *brinkmanship*? What should Khruschev do?

Source F President Kennedy's decision, 22 October 1962

> I have directed that the following initial steps be taken: first, a strict 'quarantine' on all offensive military equipment under shipment to Cuba. All ships, if found to contain cargoes of offensive weapons, will be turned back.

A Order Soviet ships to turn round.

B Send the Soviet Navy to protect the cargo ships.

C Distract the Americans – by invading West Berlin.

D Negotiate with Kennedy.

Order Soviet ships to stop.

F Order Soviet ships to go through the American blockade.

Source G Options

The screw tightens

The Soviet Union had pulled back from direct conflict but the crisis was not over. U2 photos showed that the missile sites on Cuba were nearly finished. Soviet bombers were also being assembled. Within days 80 million Americans could be killed from Cuba.

On Friday 26 October, President Kennedy got a letter from Khruschev. In it, the Soviet Union offered to remove the missiles from Cuba if Kennedy promised not to invade Cuba and to end the blockade. Above all, Khruschev made it clear he wished to avoid the horror of nuclear war. The letter offered the first hope of a peaceful solution. But the next morning a second letter arrived from Khruschev (Source **H**). It took a harder line.

Crisis point

Kennedy was confused. Which of Khruschev's letters should he believe – the first or the second? How should America respond? Turkey was a NATO ally. Kennedy would not accept a 'trade-off' of Cuban missiles for Turkish missiles. But if America attacked Cuba, might the Soviet Union do the same to Turkey?

Around the world, millions realised just how close the Great Powers were to nuclear war.

Source I   What should America do?

Robert Kennedy recalls the situation in Source **J**.

Source J   Robert Kennedy's memoirs

There were arguments – sharp disagreements. Everyone was tense, some were near exhaustion – all were weighed down with worry. I suggested that we ignore the latest Khruschev letter and respond to his earlier letter's proposal.

President Kennedy took up his brother's idea. His reply, in Source **K** accepted Khruschev's first 'offer'.

Source K   President Kennedy's proposal to the Soviet Union

1   You agree to remove weapon systems from Cuba and to halt their further introduction into Cuba.
2   We agree **a)** to remove the quarantine measures now in effect. **b)** to give assurances against an invasion of Cuba.

If the Soviet Union had not responded by Monday 29 October, America would invade Cuba. Was the world one day away from a Third World War?

Khruschev's reply came on 28 October. He accepted Kennedy's offer. The Cuban crisis was over. The world heaved a sigh of relief. On Cuba, within two months, no trace was left of the missiles of October.

Source L   Results of the crisis

Our purpose has been to help Cuba develop as its people desire. You want to relieve your country from danger. Your rockets are stationed on Turkey. You are worried about Cuba. You say it worries you because it lies at a distance of 90 miles from the United States. Turkey lies next to us!

I make this proposal. We agree to remove from Cuba offensive means (nuclear missiles). The United States on its part, will remove its similar means from Turkey.

Source H   Khruschev's proposal to Kennedy

The lessons of Cuba

Source **L** shows the lessons that America and the Soviet Union learnt as a result of the Cuban missile crisis.

● Alongside their power, America and the Soviet Union also had responsibilities towards the rest of the world.
● *Brinkmanship* (pushing each other to the brink of war) was too deadly a game to play.
● Moscow and Washington should be in closer and more direct contact – in 1963 a 'Hot line' teleprinter link was set up.
● Nuclear arms control talks should begin – in August 1963 a Test Ban Treaty was signed between America, the Soviet Union and Britain.
● Direct conflict between America and the Soviet Union, anywhere around the world, should be avoided.

Questions

1 **a)** Which option in the table on page 50 would you have advised President Kennedy to choose? Why?
  b) Which option did President Kennedy actually choose? Why?
  c) What was Kennedy's motive in choosing it?

2 **a)** What did Khruschev mean by 'as its people desire' in Source **H**?
  b) Was Khruschev's proposal reasonable?

3 Study Source **I**. How does the cartoonist show the idea of Great Power 'brinkmanship'?

4 Many American's believed that Kennedy 'won' the Missile Crisis. Would you agree?

Czechoslovakia, 1968

▶ **Why did the Soviet Union suppress reform?**
How did it keep control of one Eastern bloc satellite?

At midnight, on 20 August 1968, Ladislav Mnacko awoke. He peered out of his window. What were those shadowy shapes standing in line all along Strefanik Street? Trucks? They couldn't be ... the road was closed for repairs; nothing could be driven along it. Then he was sure. Tanks. Tanks can drive anywhere. A lot of tanks.

Czechoslovakia had been invaded (see Source **A**). Why had Czechoslovakia's allies acted to crush a fellow Warsaw Pact member and a Soviet satellite?

The 'Prague Spring'

Since the spring of 1968 the Czech Prime Minister, Alexander Dubcek, had been trying to improve living conditions in Czechoslovakia (see Source **B**).

Source A   The invasion of Czechoslovakia

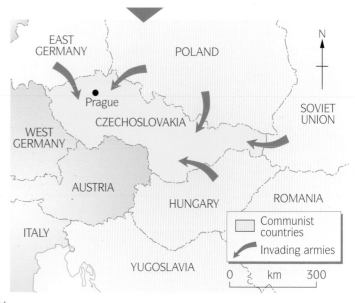

> We want to set new forces of Socialist life in motion in this country, allowing a fuller application of the advantages of Socialism.

Source B   Dubcek's ideas for Czechoslovakia, 1968

- Freedom of speech was introduced in newspapers, on the radio and on television.
- Trade with the West was developed.
- Different religions were allowed.

Dubcek's government, though still Communist, wished to take less control over people's lives. Dubcek called his ideas 'socialism with a human face'. The people of Czechoslovakia gave him their full support. The thaw in Czech Communism in early 1968 was known as the 'Prague Spring'. The Czechs tried very hard not to upset the Soviet Union. They remembered how Hungary had been crushed in 1956 (see pages 44–45). Czechoslovakia had no wish to make changes in its foreign affairs. It wished to stay a loyal ally of the Soviet Union in the Warsaw Pact.

> The word democracy is being misused. There are campaigns against honest Party workers. The aim is to end the leading role of the Party workers. The aim is to end the leading role of the Party, to undermine Socialism and to turn Czechoslovakia against other Socialist countries. Thus ... the security of our countries is threatened.

Source C   Premier Brezhnev issues his warning to Czechoslovakia in 1968

On 20 August the Warsaw Pact forces invaded Czechoslovakia with 40,000 troops. Why was the Soviet Union so frightened of change in Czechoslovakia? The Czech historian, Zeman, offers a clue in Source **D**.

The Brezhnev doctrine

Dubcek's changes were too much for Leonid Brezhnev, the Soviet leader, and other Warsaw Pact leaders. They met, and Brezhnev warned Czechoslovakia not to run the risk of opening up a 'hole' in the iron curtain (see Source **C**).

> Twice in this century the Russians have had to face an onslaught from the centre of Europe. Only they know the extent of their losses in the last war ... and the country is still governed by the men who fought in it. The Soviet Union have no intention of dismantling their defences to the West.

Source D
A Czech historian's interpretation of Soviet motives

The West was shocked by the invasion. But would the West support Czechoslovakia – or do nothing, as in Hungary in 1956?

To avoid bloodshed, the Czechs decided to offer 'passive resistance', as in Source **E**.

The campaign was organised through radio stations (see Source **F**).

As the Soviet Union took control, arrests of leading Czechs began. The Russians tried to find the broadcasters and close down their transmitters.

> Citizens – go to work normally ... keep calm ... do not give the occupation forces any excuse for armed action ... show the invaders your scorn in silence.

Source F An unknown broadcast from a Czech radio station

The Russian troops were surprised to see how much the Czechs hated them. They had believed Soviet propaganda, such as that in Source **G**.

Source G 'Tass', 21 August 1968

> Tass is authorised to state that the leaders of the Czechoslovak Socialist Republic have asked the Soviet Union and allied states to render the Czechoslovak people urgent assistance. This request was brought about by the threat which has arisen to the Socialist system, existing in Czechoslovakia.

Later the Russian leader, Brezhnev, justified Soviet action (see Source **H**).

Other satellites in Eastern Europe took careful note of this idea, which came to be known as 'the Brezhnev Doctrine'. Alexander Dubcek was flown to Moscow. For days Czech and Soviet leaders talked. On 27 August the Czech leaders returned from Moscow.

Source I Alexander Dubcek's response to 'The Prague Spring' was to announce that he thought it necessary for the Czech people to face reality

> To normalise the present complex situation ... it will be necessary to take measures limiting freedom of expression as we have become accustomed to it.

Source E A Czech demonstrator offers 'passive resistance' to a Soviet tank

> When forces that are hostile to Socialism try to turn the development of some Socialist country towards capitalism ... it becomes not only a problem of the country concerned, but a common problem and concern of all Socialist countries.

Source H Leonid Brezhnev's comment on the Czech uprising

The aftermath

Soviet troops were allowed to stay in Czechoslovakia. Censorship was brought back. The heavy hand of Moscow once more gripped Czechoslovakia. A Czech student, Jan Palach, set fire to himself in the centre of Prague as a protest.

In April 1969 Dubcek resigned. His idea of making Czechoslovakian Communism more human lay in ruins.

Questions

1 Explain what was meant by the 'Prague Spring'.

2 Why was the Soviet Union so unwilling to allow Czechoslovakia to make its internal reforms (Sources **C** and **D**)?

3 What does Source **E** reveal about Czech 'passive resistance'?

4 What was 'the Brezhnev Doctrine'?

8 Great Power flashpoints in the Far East

Friends and enemies

▶ *How did the Great Powers view one another in the Far East?*
What was 'The Domino Theory'?

The Korean War made East and West distrust each other even more. After it, the Cold War became a worldwide matter, rather than a European one. In the Far East, the East–West conflict was complicated. America faced the combined strength of the two Communist giants.

Friends: the Soviet Union and China

Before the Korean War, the Soviet Union and China had signed a Treaty of Friendship (Source **A**).

Soviet aid flooded into China after 1950. Soviet experts masterminded China's first Five-Year Plan. Source **B** shows a massive new bridge being built over the River Yangtsze. It was one of over 200 industrial projects in China built by the Soviet Union. By the mid 1950s, 10,000 Soviet experts were working in China and 10,000 Chinese were being trained in the Soviet Union. Half of China's trade was with the Soviet Union.

How does this scene portray contrasts in Communist culture between China and the Soviet Union?

The Soviet Union loaned China 2,000 million dollars to help fight the Korean War. It seemed as if the two Communist giants were thinking and acting as one.

Source C Mao spoke of the relationship with the Soviet Union

We belong to the front headed by the Soviet Union.

In 1956 Khruschev sought Mao's advice before acting against Hungary. Khruschev, for his part, warned America in no uncertain terms (see Source **D**).

Source D Nikita Khruschev's warning to America, 1956

An attack on the People's Republic of China is an attack on the Soviet Union.

The USSR will give credits to China to the amount of 300,000,000 US dollars – used for payments for deliveries from the Soviet Union of equipment and materials (for electric power stations, engineering plants, mining equipment, railways and other transport equipment).

Source A Extract from the Treaty of Friendship, 14 February 1950

Source B A new bridge across the River Yangtze

The West had further cause for concern when, in 1957, the Soviet Union promised to supply China with nuclear weapons. China's communist leader Mao Tse Tung was certain that Soviet missile strength, linked with China's manpower, would prove to be an unbeatable combination against America. Mao believed that nothing could stop the eventual spread of Communism.

Enemies: America's actions

After Korea, America lost no time in getting together friendly countries in South East Asia. With America's help they would defend the area in case of Communist expansion. The result was SEATO (the South East Asia Treaty Organisation). America confirmed its support by signing a Peace Treaty with Japan. In February 1955 America signed a defence treaty with Nationalist China. An American fleet protected Formosa (Taiwan). Chiang Kaishek, the leader of mainland China before Mao, was kept in power with massive amounts of America aid, much to Communist China's disgust.

America still saw Mao as a 'puppet' of the Soviet Union, directed by Moscow. America badly misjudged the facts. Mao's Communism was different to Moscow's. America tried to isolate China at the United Nations, through trade and politics. China turned events more towards the Soviet Union.

Source F The Domino Theory

China's threats

China did have a genuine wish to spread Communism throughout South East Asia. If necessary, this would be achieved by aggression (partly in response to the American threat).

In South East Asia it was this Chinese version of Communism that posed the greatest threat to America.

Source E Mao Tse Tung had made his position clear

> Violent Revolution is accomplished by the power of the gun.

America's risky idea of 'brinkmanship' (going to the brink of war by threat to force the enemy to retreat) had paid off.

If one 'domino' was allowed to fall to Communism, others would fall as well. This state of affairs was recognised by President Eisenhower (see Source **G**).

Source G President Eisenhower

> The loss of any single country in South East Asia could lead to the loss of all Asia, then India and Japan, finally endangering the security of Europe.

The 'Domino Theory'

Mao's threats worried Americans. They saw the Chinese as a 'Yellow Peril', which would sweep across South East Asia, spreading revolution. America warned China that she would not be allowed to expand. When, in 1955, China tried to gain some off-shore islands, America threatened to use tactical nuclear weapons. The Chinese backed down.

America thought back to Korea. Had that been the first domino? Only strong American action had held it upright.

Fed by constant propaganda, the Domino Theory took root in American minds. America was determined to support South East Asia, whenever and whichever 'dominoes' were threatened.

---

1 Why did the Soviet Union supply aid to China after 1949?

2 Which two sources confirm the friendship of China and the Soviet Union?

3 a) How did America try to isolate China? What was the result of these attempts?
b) Why might Mao's words in Source **E** worry America?
c) How did America react to China's attempt to expand in 1955?

4 a) What steps did America take to contain the spread of Communism in South East Asia after 1953?
b) Explain, in your own words, what the 'Domino Theory' was.
c) Which country, in America's view, might have been the first domino?
d) What might any future dangers be, for America, of the 'Domino Theory'?

55

The Sino-Soviet split

▶ *Why did the two Communist Great Powers fall out?*
How did the Chinese and Soviet styles of Communism differ?

Friends into enemies

America's concerns about the Far East were largely based on the 'two against one' situation shown in Source **A**.

Source A Cartoon showing China and the Soviet Union in league against the snarling tiger – America

Throughout the 1950s this was the situation that existed. China and the Soviet Union were close friends as the Treaty of Friendship, in Source **B**, shows.

Source B Extract from the Treaty of Friendship, 14 October 1954

The friendly relations between the USSR and China will be the basis of close co-operation … founded on the sincere desire to assist one another to strengthen ties of brotherly friendship.

The Soviet Union helped China to modernise her military forces, farming and factories.

In 1954 the Soviet Union had also promised to help China develop nuclear weapons. Yet, only three years later, China exploded its first nuclear bomb, to be followed – as Source **C** shows – with a much more powerful hydrogen bomb.

Source C The mushroom cloud created by the explosion of China's first hydrogen bomb, 17 June 1967

What was so surprising was that China developed its own nuclear weapons, without the Soviet Union's help. The Chinese leader, Mao Zedong, realised how significant this was (see Source **D**).

Source D Extract from proclamation by Mao Tse Tung

We are now in fourth place in the world. This is the result of Khrushev's 'help'. He forced us to take our own road. We should give him a big medal.

Causes of the split

China would never rely on the Soviet Union again. The two Communist giants seemed more like enemies than friends. What had caused the Sino (Chinese)-Soviet split?

Even before Mao gained power in 1949 there had been disagreements. In the Chinese Civil War, Stalin gave Mao only lukewarm support against Chiang Kaishek. After Mao came to power there was a 'honeymoon period' of friendship with the Soviet Union which lasted until 1955 (see pages 24–25). Even then, there were problems.

One cause of tension was the Soviet view of Mao and China. Stalin treated China as just another Soviet satellite, like Hungary or Poland. Mao respected Stalin, but he would not be Moscow's puppet. He was determined to take an independent line. But in order to modernise, China did need the Soviet Union's aid and advice.

In 1956, Kruschev's speech against Stalin sent shock waves to Peking. Mao disagreed with Khruschev. Mao thought that Stalin had been a good leader of the Communist world. Was Khruschev's attack on Stalin's leadership a sideways dig at the similar style of Mao in China?

Rival views of Communism

Mao and Stalin thought about Communism in different ways. This, in turn, led to quarrels between the two men. Mao knew that Chinese Communism relied upon the ongoing support of the peasants. Stalin could never understand this, so his advice – in Mao's eyes – was incorrect.

Mao also disagreed with the Soviet Union on the best means to spread Communist ideas to other countries. Mao thought that the Soviet Union used Communism as a world struggle, involving violent revolutions. He saw himself as the true follower of Karl Marx and Lenin.

In contrast, Mao thought that Khruschev's ideas of 'peaceful co-existence' with America were totally wrong. To Mao, America was just a 'paper tiger', strong in theory, but weak in practice. The Korean War seemed to prove this. Mao wished to take a hard line against the West. Khruschev, for his part, thought that Mao's views were dangerous.

Finally, Mao felt insulted by Khruschev's boast that only the Soviet Union and America, and not China, were the only 'true' World Powers.

The split worsens

Relations between China and the Soviet Union became more and more strained. In 1958 the Soviet Union condemned Mao's 'Great Leap Forward' plan to modernise Chinese industry. The Soviet Union opinion of Mao's plan is shown in Source **E**.

In 1960 the Soviet Union withdrew its aid and its technical experts from China. Half-finished factories were left to rust. Khruschev also tore up the agreement to share nuclear weapons with China. Military aid from the Soviet Union to China stopped. Trade between the two was affected.

The split becomes known

In 1963 Mao made the split public. Each side poured out hostile propaganda in speeches, radio broadcasts, posters and newspapers (see Source **F**).

The split between the Soviet Union and China divided the whole Communist world. Sixty-five out of 86 Communist parties took the Soviet Union's side. The Chinese were forced to rely even more on their own efforts and resources.

In 1969, Chinese troops killed 31 Soviet guards in a dispute over where part of the 45,000 mile frontier between the two countries should run. The crisis passed, but each side now feared the other. The Chinese feared the Soviet Union's nuclear strength and rushed to build nuclear shelters. For their part, the Soviet Union feared China's vast army and aggressive leaders.

By 1970 the 'two against one' line-up was in tatters. Now there was a 'triangle' of world powers.

> A road of dangerous experiment, a road of disregard for the experience of other socialist (Communist) states.

Source E Khruschev's view of Mao's Great Leap Forward

Source F An example of Chinese propaganda from the *People's Daily*, Peking, 4 June 1967

> Throughout the past year scarcely a day has passed without Brezhnev and Kosygin attacking China's great revolution. A tragedy has taken place in international Communism. Its creators are the scabs – Kruschev, Brezhnev and Kosygin …

Questions

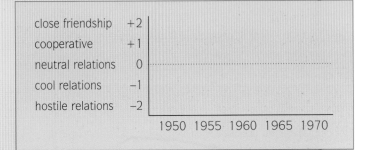

1 a) Copy out a large version of the graph below. Now use the information on pages 24–25 and 56–57 to plot the changes in Sino-Soviet relations (1950–70).

close friendship	+2	
cooperative	+1	
neutral relations	0	
cool relations	–1	
hostile relations	–2	
		1950 1955 1960 1965 1970

b) Use your graph to write an account of relations between China and Soviet Union, 1950–70.

2 Why did China's leaders fall out with the Soviet Union?

Vietnam: a new domino

 Why did America fight the Vietnam War?

Background

The table opposite charts Vietnam's fortunes between 1900 and 1954.

The Great Powers met at Geneva in Switzerland to decide what to do. Source **A** shows the outcome of these talks, and the events which followed.

Source A Vietnam 1954–60

Factfile: Vietnam	
1900–45	Vietnam part of French Indo-China.
1941–45	Vietnam occupied by Japan during Second World War. Ho Chi Minh – a Communist – organised 'Vietminh' to drive out Japanese. Vietminh aided by America.
1945	Vietnam wished to be independent nation.
1945	French sent military forces to reclaim Indo-China. Bitter 'Guerilla War'.
1949	Vietminh gained support of Mao and Chinese Communists.
	America agreed to support France against a 'Domino Falling'.
1954	Major defeat for France at Dien Bein Phu. French surrender. Peace talks.

1954
Geneva decisions:
1 Vietnam split into two.
2 Dividing line 17°N.
3 Free elections to reunite Vietnam by 1956.
4 Cambodia, Laos: independent, neutral states.
5 All foreign troops to be withdrawn.

1954
Ho Chi Minh sets up Communist government in North. Confident of uniting Vietnam in elections.

1954
Government of South Vietnam set up – led by President Diem.

1954
Communist supporters in South trained in guerilla warfare by North Vietnamese.

1954
America fears Communist success in elections. Supports South.

1955
American 'advisers' take over South Vietnam's armed forces. CIA step up operation against Vietcong in South.

1959–60
South Vietnamese Government unpopular. Vietcong win peasant support in countryside. In towns Vietcong mount bomb attacks against political enemies.

1958–59
Increased Vietcong guerila activity in South.

1956–57
America continues to support Diem – although his government corrupt, less democratic, more military support given.

America acts

To America, Vietnam looked like another Asian 'domino'. America would have had to help South Vietnam against the Communist North, or risk South East Asia falling under Communist control.

Meanwhile, Ho Chi Minh's Communist Government sent supplies and encouragement to the Communist guerilla force – the *Vietcong* – fighting in the South.

Massive amounts of American arms and money failed to stop the spread of Vietcong influence. In 1961 President Kennedy decided to send military advisors to South Vietnam. By 1962 there were 16,500 troops in Vietnam, assisting South Vietnamese troops against the Vietcong. In 1964 the new American President, Lyndon Johnson, declared his determination not to 'lose Vietnam' to Communism.

Escalation

Johnson decided to *escalate* (greatly increase) the American presence in Vietnam. Within 18 months, America was involved in a full-scale land and air war. Its air force pounded military targets and Vietcong supply routes.

Aerial tactics: Factfile

- Helicopter gunships, jets and heavy bombers were used.
- In five years, 1965–70, more bombs were dropped on North Vietnam than in the Second World War.
- Chemical weapons were used like napalm, designed to set fire and burn targets.
- To reveal the whereabouts of the Vietcong and their supply routes, the dense tree cover of the jungle was sprayed with poisonous chemicals such as 'Agent Orange'.

The Americans faced a determined enemy. By 1968 the British journalist James Cameron, whilst in Vietnam, doubted the success of America's tactics.

Every aspect of life is dominated by this mood of siege ... air raid shelters, rifles stacked at the corners of paddy fields, great posters, aircraft recognition charts, weapon identifications 'roccet', 'bom' ... When arms drills were signalled they were taken deadly seriously.

There was a sense of outrage. By what right do these airmen intrude over a country with which they are not formally at war? Who gave these people the sanction to drop their bombs on roads, bridges, houses, to blow up the harvest, to destroy people of whom they know nothing? Would this sort of thing blow Communism out of their heads?

Source B James Cameron questions American tactics

Despite the bombing, North Vietnam continued to supply the Vietcong in South Vietnam with ever-increasing amounts of aid. Often, these supplies came down the 'Ho Chi Minh Trail' which ran from the North and on into South Vietnam.

'Hearts and minds'

President Johnson hoped for a 'quick kill'. But the tactics of America's land forces in South Vietnam were based on several errors of judgement:

First, America believed that it could 'win' the war in Vietnam. France had already tried and failed, but President Johnson could 'simply not believe that the US could be defeated by a bunch of guerilas in black pyjamas'.

Secondly, the Vietcong were experienced and dedicated. Their tactics – mounting ambushes and raids from secret jungle hideouts – often at night, were extremely successful.

Thirdly, Americans were told to fight for 'the hearts and minds' of the Vietnamese. But how would the peasants react to events such as those described by an American soldier who was involved (see Source **C**)?

Off to the right a woman's head appeared from some bushes. All the GIs started firing at her. The bullets riddled the woman's body. The men were oblivious to everything but slaughter. They just kept shooting at her. You could see the bones flying in the air, chip by chip.

Source C Evidence submitted in the trial of Lieutenant William Calley, accused of murdering 20 Vietnamese civilians at Mylai, March 1971

Initially, American politicians thought that 'victory' in Vietnam was worth any sacrifice. But in a decade of fighting, America would come to realise its errors of judgement – the hard way.

Questions

1. Explain who the Vietminh and the Vietcong were.

2. Imagine you are one of the following people. Describe how you feel about the fighting in Vietnam and the American involvement in the war.
   a) a North Vietnamese peasant.
   b) a South Vietnamese peasant.
   c) an American GI.

Vietnam: America's agony

▶ *What role did the media play in changing American public opinion?*
What was the result of the American withdrawal?
What were the long-term effects of the war?

Body counts and body bags

Despite American 'escalation' the war dragged on. By 1969, over half a million US troops were in Vietnam. The costs of the war were colossal – over 28 billion a year – more than Johnson's entire American welfare programme. Meanwhile, casualties rose by 1969; 160 young men died per week. Their remains returning to America for burial in body bags (see Source **A**) were a powerful and upsetting symbol of America's failure in Vietnam.

Source A The American army in Vietnam, attending to the wounded and the dead

To replace the losses, unpopular Draft Laws were passed to force young men to serve in Vietnam. With no 'victory' in sight, many Americans became unsure about why their troops were in Vietnam in the first place.

The television war

The horrors of Vietnam were shown nightly in homes across America through colour TV news reports. Millions were repulsed by the screenings of 'search and destroy' missions (Source **B**) and became familiar with terms like 'fire fights' and 'body counts'.

Source B Vietnam search and destroy mission

At first, American politicians suffered from an 'arrogance of power'. They thought that victory was worth any sacrifice. But was there a limit to the cost, and losses of men, that the American people would accept?

The protest movement

With 50,000 dead and the weekly 'body count' rising to 300 deaths, American public opinion began to turn against the War. By the late 1960s there were peace protesters demonstrating outside the White House.

Protests took many forms, such as art, poems, articles and popular songs (see Source **E**).

Source C
Peace protesters

▶ Hey, hey, LBJ! How many kids did you kill today?

One does not use napalm (*a chemical weapon which inflicts terrible burns*) on villages and hamlets sheltering civilians ... if one is attempting to persuade these people of the rightness of one's cause. One does not blast hamlets to dust with high explosives from jet planes miles in the sky without warning – if one is attempting to woo the people living there to the goodness of one's cause ... One does not defoliate (*destroy vegetation in*) a country and deform its people with chemicals if one is attempting to persuade them of the foe's evil nature.

Source D Richard Hammer, an eye-witness, comments

Source E Extracts from 'John Brown', by Bob Dylan, 1963

John Brown went off to war to fight on foreign shore.
His mam sure was proud of him!
He stood straight and tall in his uniform and all.
His mama's face broke out all in a grin.
Oh son, you look so fine, I'm glad you're a son of mine,
You make me proud to know you hold a gun
Do what the captain says, lots of medals you will get,
And we'll put them on the wall when you come home.

Then a letter finally came saying, 'Go down and meet the train.
Your son's a-coming home from the war.'
She smiled and went right down, she looked everywhere around
But she could not see her soldier son in sight.
But as all the people passed, she saw her son at last,
When she did she could hardly believe her eyes.
Oh his face was all shot up and his hand was all blow off
And he wore a metal brace around his waist.
He whispered kind of slow, in a voice she did not know,
While she couldn't even recognise his face!

'Don't you remember, Ma, when I went off to war
You thought it was the best thing I could do?
I was on the battleground, you were home … acting proud.
You wasn't there standing in my shoes.'
'Oh, and I thought when I was there, God, what am I doing here?
I'm a-tryin' to kill somebody or die tryin'.
But the thing that scared me most was when my enemy came close
And I saw that his face looked just like mine.'

As he turned away to walk, his Ma was still in shock
At seein' the metal brace that helped him stand.
But as he turned to go, he called his mother close
And he dropped his medals down into her hand.'

Other well-known individuals like Muhammed Ali, the world heavy-weight boxing champion, protested by refusing the Army Draft.

Across America many students held 'anti-War' sit-ins and marches – some of which ended in riots. At times their protests ended in violence; with the authorities killing demonstrating students. By 1968 more Americans opposed the Vietnam War than supported it.

In Vietnam, eye-witness commentators such as Richard Hammer reinforced public opinion (see Source **D**).

One political casuality was 'LBJ' himself; whose unpopularity forced his withdrawal from the Presidential election.

American withdrawal

The new President, Richard Nixon, swept to power with key policies for changing America's involvement in Vietnam.

- A promise to 'bring the boys back home'.
- 'Vietnamisation' to hand the conduct of the War to South Vietnamese troops.
- An attempt to reach 'peace with honour' through a peace agreement with North Vietnam at Peace Talks began in Paris in 1968.

'Vietnamisation' saw a reduction in American forces from 1969, but not an end to the War. The Peace Talks dragged on for five years. Meanwhile, with the Communist forces closing in, Nixon felt forced to bomb supply routes in Cambodia and Laos as well as North Vietnam. Eventually, through Henry Kissinger's efforts, a ceasefire was agreed. In 1973 the last American troops withdrew from Vietnam. Within months fighting broke out again. South Vietnam failed to hold out against the Vietcong. In May 1975 the Communists captured Saigon and renamed it Ho Chi Minh City. Shortly after, other Communist forces also took over much of Cambodia and Laos.

Wars have no winners; both sides paid a heavy price.

Questions

1 Which sources – visual Sources **A** and **B**, written Source **D** or aural Source **E** – might have had the most powerful impact in America?

2 How significant were **a)** the media, **b)** anti-war protesters, and **c)** 'draft-dodgers' in changing American public opinion?

3 Did American public opinion alter the course of the Vietnam War?

4 How successful was Richard Nixon in achieving his aims over Vietnam?

9 A decade of détente: 1970s

Motives and methods

▶ **What caused the Great Powers to seek an easing of tension?**
What forms of cooperation did détente take?
Was the desire for détente simply based on self-interest?

Motives and methods

Despite their Great Power status the Soviet Union, China and America had all learnt hard lessons about the limit of their powers. Each had suffered major setbacks – the Soviet Union over Cuba, America over Vietnam and China over the Soviet Union.

Was the time right for a change in relations between East and West? In which areas might they seek to cooperate? The Great Powers could:

- reduce the arms race and cut back on nuclear weapons;
- stop direct interference in each other's affairs;
- develop face to face contact between Great Power leaders;
- re-create the idea of 'Summit Meetings';
- encourage friendship and cooperation at other levels; in science, economics, trade, sport and culture.

The ten years from 1969 to 1979 became the decade of *détente* (a French word meaning 'a relaxation of tension' between states). During these years America and the Soviet Union made efforts to reduce the areas of tension between them. At the same time, China and America worked hard to create a measure of friendship to replace their 20 years of hostility. Each Great Power had very different reasons for wanting détente (see table below). How far did each Great Power seek détente simply out of 'self-interest'?

Though détente saw East–West tension ease, relations between China and the Soviet Union stayed poor. Their quarrel left each Communist giant isolated. This helped the cause of détente. Both China and the Soviet Union wished to be on good terms with America, not least for fear of what their Communist neighbour might do.

Great Power motives for détente		
America	**The Soviet Union**	**China**
• To drive a wedge between the Soviet Union and China. • This would be to America's advantage in the fight against Communism in Vietnam (because the Soviet Union and China cooperated in supplying North Vietnam with arms). • America's leaders – President Nixon and Secretary of State, Henry Kissinger – were keen to set up realistic working relations with Moscow and Peking.	• President Brezhnev was keen to extend Khruschev's idea of 'peaceful co-existence'. • Brezhnev saw détente as a way to increase Soviet trade with the West and so develop the Soviet Union's economy in order to improve living standards within the Soviet Union. • To decrease defence spending. • To persuade the West to accept the post-war situation in Eastern Europe. • To avoid the Soviet Union being the odd one out in the '2 against 1' line up: America, the Soviet Union and China. The Soviet Union was keen to create better relations with America.	• Her motives were forced upon her by the actions of the other two Great Powers. • America had been hostile to China – her policy in South East Asia first over Korea, then Vietnam worried China. • Ever since the 1960 split with the Soviet Union, China feared the Soviet Union. China looked to America for friendship to isolate the Soviet Union. • China's leaders wanted to modernise the country – especially farming, industry, science, technology and defence. Increased trade with the West would help to modernise China more quickly.

The costs of defence

Nowhere was this self-interest more obvious than in the desire to reduce the spiralling costs of the Arms Race. By 1968, 41% of America's yearly wealth was spent on the armed forces. Yet Vietnam and Cuba had revealed the military limitations of the Great Powers.

The Great Power leaders: Nixon, Brezhnev and Mao realised that money diverted from defence spending could develop their own economies and improve standards of living at home.

Helsinki

The high point of American–Soviet détente was the Helsinki Agreement of 1975. At Helsinki, in Finland, 35 states, including America and the Soviet Union, agreed that the frontiers of post-1945 Europe should be permanent. This pleased the Soviet Union. The Helsinki Agreement was interpreted differently by the key nations involved. The Soviet Union thought it meant that the West accepted the iron curtain as a fact of life and that Soviet influence in Eastern Europe could not be questioned. It was also agreed, at the demand of America's President Carter, that all states should respect 'human rights' such as freedom of thought and religion. By this, the West hoped that people in Communist countries would be given more freedom to express their views, without fear of arrest or imprisonment.

SALT 1

Both America and the Soviet Union remained locked in a vastly expensive Nuclear Arms Race. But America was falling behind. In conventional armed strength, the Soviet-controlled Warsaw Pact forces in Europe easily outnumbered the NATO forces. As Source **A** suggests, the cost of the arms race was colossal.

In 1969 America and the Soviet Union began SALT talks (Strategic Arms Limitation Talks). The aim was to slow down the arms race by limiting the construction of new middle-range nuclear weapons. Covered in the talks were ICBMs (Inter-Continental Ballistic Missiles – long-range missiles), SLBMs (Submarine Launched Ballistic Missiles) and ABMs (Anti-Ballistic Missile defences). The number of land and submarine missiles and aircraft able to deliver nuclear warheads was frozen.

The Soviet Union was allowed to have more missiles, in total, than America. This was because many American missiles were capable of carrying several warheads, each aimed at separate targets. Each side was only allowed to have 100 ABMs on each of two sites. This cut down defence costs for both countries, since a complete shield of ABMs was almost impossible and very expensive. Each side was allowed to use spy satellites to check that the other was not breaking the arms limits. SALT was signed in 1972.

Despite the SALT agreement, the arms race continued.

SALT 2

Since the SALT agreement was only for five years, further talks were needed. SALT 2 began, first with President Nixon, then Ford and then Carter. The new talks were very complicated. America and Russia were trying to agree on arms limits involving new weapons not covered by SALT 1.

Although SALT 2 was signed in June 1979, world events took a hand. The whole process of détente was thrown into confusion when, on Christmas Day 1979, the Soviet Union invaded Afghanistan.

Cooperation between America and the Soviet Union was at an end. The SALT 2 agreement was forgotten. Détente was over.

Source A
US cartoon, 1970

Questions

1 Were the Great Power motives for détente based only on self-interest?

2 Explain why, and how, the years 1969–79 developed into the decade of détente. Your essay will need an *introduction*, where you briefly set the scene; a *development*, where you explain the 'how' and 'why'; and a brief *conclusion*. Here you should write your opinion of détente. First organise these jumbled-up headings into a good structure (**a–e**) for an essay.

   a) Détente between China and America.
   b) Why each Great Power wanted détente.
   c) Why détente ended.
   d) The practical results of détente.
   e) Détente between America and Russia.

10 A return to the Cold War: 1980s

World friendships and flashpoints

▶ **How did the Great Powers seek to 'win friends and influence people'?**
What were the effects of such strategies?

The era of detente did not end the deep *ideological* differences between East and West. Instead, East and West grew to recognise another's' 'sphere of influence'. Both America and the Soviet Union sought new allies on a worldwide scale (Source **A**).

Source A   Map showing Great Power friendships and flashpoints

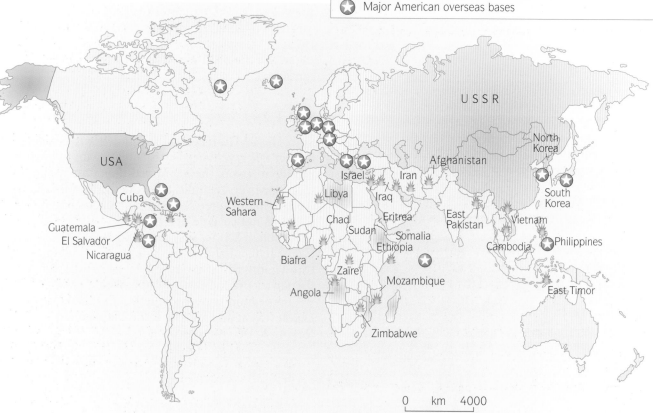

▦	Areas of strong Communist influence (troops, aid, etc)
▦	America
✸	Major wars/conflicts
★	Major American overseas bases

The 'Cold War neutrality' was retained – nowhere did American troops fight Soviet soldiers face to face. Yet, as Source **B** shows, Great Power influence made the whole world a potential battleground.

Great Power presence

One anecdote from personal experience will serve to illustrate the worldwide Great Power presence.

Factfile on 1983

- 164 countries
- 45 countries fighting
- 40 different wars
- 20 countries at war supplied by American weapons
- 13 countries at war supplied by Soviet weapons

Source B Author's recollections of the American presence in East Anglia in the 1970s and 80s

Source C American marines invading Grenada, October 1983

I started teaching in Suffolk in the 1970s and 80s. …The skies were full of the sights and sounds of the US Air Force going about their Cold War business. Phantom fighter jets, Jolly Green Giant helicopters and, later, ground-attack 'Tank busters' flew in and out of the nearby large NATO base at Bentwaters. …

Around Ipswich many American cars could be seen and many American accents could be heard. The American base provided jobs for many local people. … Elsewhere, several other large American bases were fully operational – Woodbridge, Mildenhall, Alconbury … In those days, East Anglia almost felt like America's fifty-first state.'

Great Power actions, like those in Source **C**, were not popular with everybody. Compare Sources **D** and **E** which are two accounts of the American actions in Grenada.

The tiny Caribbean island nation of Grenada leapt into international headlines on 25 October when a force of 2,100 US and Caribbean troops stormed ashore to overthrow the government, itself recently installed after a coup. Artillery and infantry attacks brought the US a swift victory, though scattered groups of troops took days to be rounded up. The attack was prompted by neighbouring island states who feared that the new regime was backed by Cuba and Russia. When the fighting was over, papers showing that such links existed were found.

Extract from R. Matthews, *Eyewitness to the 80s: A Moment in Time*, Ted Smart, 1990

Source D An account of the American actions in Grenada

On 13 March, 1979 the opposition carried out a bloodless coup and seized power. … Because of the government's socialist ideology, there was constant harassment from the United States which did everything possible to destabilise the Grenadian government. … The government based its foreign policy on the principles of anti-imperialism and non-alignment. Special attention was given to the development of ties with the socialist world.

The US then began to take definite steps towards military intervention. … Early in the morning of 25 October 1983, 5,000 marines and Green Berets landed on the island. They were followed several hours later by a symbolic contingent of 300 policemen from six Caribbean countries; … who joined the farce of a 'multi-national intervention for humanitarian reasons'.

Resistance from the Grenadian militia and some Cuban technicians and workers, meant that the operation lasted much longer than expected. The US suffered combat casualties and the press was barred from entering Grenada until all resistance had been eliminated. This made it impossible to verify how many civilians had been killed. …

Extract from R. Bissio (ed.), *The World: A Third World Guide 1995/96*, Instituto del Tercer Mundo, Uruguay, 1995

Source E Another account

Questions

1 Undertake an enquiry into how either America or the Soviet Union developed their respective spheres of influence through:
   • the 'friendship war'
   • overseas bases
   • the arms trade
   • supporting civil wars.

2 Compare Sources **D** and **E**.
   Complete a copy of the chart opposite.

		Source D	Source E
Facts	Similar		
Facts	Different		
Opinions	'Pro-American' words, phrases.		
Opinions	'Anti-American' words, phrases.		

Afghanistan: Brezhnev's Vietnam

Why did the Soviet Union fail to subdue the Afghan rebels? Can comparisons be drawn between Afghanistan and Vietnam in terms of the Great Powers?

Background

As Source **A** shows, Afghanistan holds an important strategic position in military, economic and political senses.

Although Afghanistan was a founder member of the non-aligned states of Africa and Asia, the Soviet Union had – for many years – supported Communist governments which were friendly towards the Soviet Union.

Unrest

After a Muslim revolution in neighbouring Iran (see Source **A**), extreme Muslim freedom fighters, the Mujahedin, created a very unstable situation in Afghanistan. They attempted to remove their anti-Muslim, pro-Soviet Prime Minister, through waging a guerilla war.

Premier Brezhnev faced a difficult decision. If the rebels succeeded in Afghanistan, there was a danger that pro-Muslim and anti-Communist ideas might spread to the Soviet Union. Soviet troops could be sent in to destroy the rebels and 'prop up' the Communist government. Brezhnev had used this strategy before, with success, in Czechoslovakia in 1968 (see page 52). Now though, the situation was more complicated. America had warned the Soviet Union not to invade Afghanistan. Soviet aggression might destroy the whole process of détente between the Great Powers. As Source **B** shows, whatever Brezhnev decided, the image of the Soviet Union as a Great Power would be certain to suffer.

Invasion

Over Christmas 1979, events moved quickly, as the time chart at the top of page 67 shows.

Source A Afghanistan and its neighbours

> **Iran**
> In 1974 the Ayotollah Khomeini took power. He set up an Islamic republic in Iran. All aspects of western life were removed from the country. He regarded America as evil.

> **Soviet Union**
> The southern parts of the Soviet Union were mainly Muslim. Their population was rising quickly. Brezhnev feared that they might become 'infected' with Iran's Muslim, anti-Communist political ideas.

> **Afghanistan**
> Poor, remote mountainous. Until 1979 pro-Soviet. Politically unsettled.

> **Oil**
> Oil fields on which West depends

> **American Aid to Afghanistan**
> Rebels came through Pakistan. America claimed that the Soviet army in Afghanistan was a threat to American oil supplies.

> **Oil supplies**
> Oil to America, Europe, Japan

Iran, Iraq, Soviet Union, Afghanistan, Kabul, Pakistan, Saudi Arabia

0   km   1000

Source B Alex Bovin, writing in *Izvestia*, a Soviet newspaper, in 1980, justified Brezhnev's decision to invade

> The Soviet Union was forced to make a choice; we had to bring in troops or let the Afghan revolution be defeated. We knew that the decision to bring in troops would not be popular, even if it was legal. But we also knew that we would have ceased to be a great power if we (did not take) unpopular but necessary decisions.

Reaction

Criticism of the Soviet Union's actions was immediate and worldwide. Afghanistan's Muslim neighbours objected. America feared these actions as the start of Soviet expansion into Southern Asia.

Ignoring the protests, the Soviet Union stayed. By February 1980 there were 80,000 Soviet troops in Afghanistan. The troops were supposed to fight alongside the Afghan army to root out the Muslim rebels. But, just as America learnt to its cost in Vietnam, the reality differed.

- The Afghan army was inefficient.
- The Mujahedin forces, such as those in Source **C**, fought using guerilla tactics and inflicted heavy losses in the remote country areas used as Soviet supply routes. By avoiding set battles they proved very difficult to defeat.
- The rebels' motivation was high since they were fighting to turn Afghanistan into a Muslim country.
- The Mujahedin were well equipped with weapons supplied from America and China which also objected to the Soviet actions.

The Soviet Union was forced to send in increased numbers of troops. Yet still they were unable to defeat the Mujahedin who captured Soviet equipment and prisoners; some of whom were executed.

Effects

As the years went by and Soviet casualties and costs of the War mounted, the Soviet Union came under increasing pressure to withdraw. Estimates of the Soviet soldiers killed ranged from 13,000 to 20,000 troops. As Source **D** reveals, some soldiers failed to see the point of fighting in Afghanistan.

Source D   One Soviet soldier's opinion of his time spent in Afghanistan

We were given medals which we don't wear. When the time comes we'll return them. Those medals (were) received ... in a dishonest war.

Time chart

24 December	Soviet troops captured Kabul airport.
27 December	Soviet army cross northern border into Afghanistan.
28 December	Premier Brezhnev informs American President Carter that Soviet troops had been 'invited in' to protect country.
	KGB squad assassinated Prime Minister Amin.
1 January	New Communist government set up, under Barak Karmal.

Source C   Mujahedin rebels

As ever, Afghanistan and its people suffered worst of all. Between 500,000 and one million died. By 1989 half its population were homeless. Insufficient food could be grown to feed those who survived the war.

Questions

1. Why did the Soviet Union invade Afghanistan?

2. Why wasn't the Soviet invasion of Afghanistan as successful as that in Czechoslovakia and Hungary?

3. Study Source **B**. How far do you agree with Bovin's views?

4. Why were the Mujahedin so successful against the Soviet invasion?

5. **a)** Compare the Soviet Union's experiences in Afghanistan with the American experience in Vietnam (see pages 58–61).
   b) Draw a Concept Map to plot the similarities, links and connections.

A new arms race?

► **What was the impact of the invasion of Afghanistan upon Great Power relations?**
How responsible was Ronald Reagan for the new arms race?

Source A Reagan's view of the world

Introduction

The Soviet Union's invasion of Afghanistan destroyed Great Power détente. The American Congress refused to agree to the nuclear arms limits within the SALT 2 terms.

In protest, America *boycotted* the Moscow Olympics of 1980. Later, economic *sanctions* were applied, for instance agreements to export American grain to the Soviet Union were cancelled.

Reagan and the 'Evil Empire'

In 1980 Ronald Reagan was elected as President of the USA. He promised to make America strong. Throughout his life Reagan had been opposed to Communism (see Source **B**). Although he seemed, at times, to have a simplistic grasp of world affairs, as Source **A** suggests, as one of the World's most powerful men his views were important.

Source B In March 1983 Reagan accused the Soviet Union of being an 'evil empire'

► The focus of evil in the modern world ... I believe that Communism is another, sad, bizarre chapter in human history whose last pages even now are being written.

A 'new' Cold War

With the end of détente, the two Superpowers entered into yet another round of the nuclear arms race. This led the early 1980s to be regarded as a new phase in the Cold War.

America and her NATO allies were also concerned about the development of new Soviet weapons, not included in any arms limitation talks.

The Soviet Union, experience shows, is willing to threaten or use force beyond its own frontiers – Afghanistan ... shows this clearly. The Soviet Union is devoting ... a large part of its resources to a massive military build-up, far exceeding its defence needs.

Source C According to NATO

Reagan planned to undermine Communism in different ways, shown in Source **D**, at different levels and in different places.

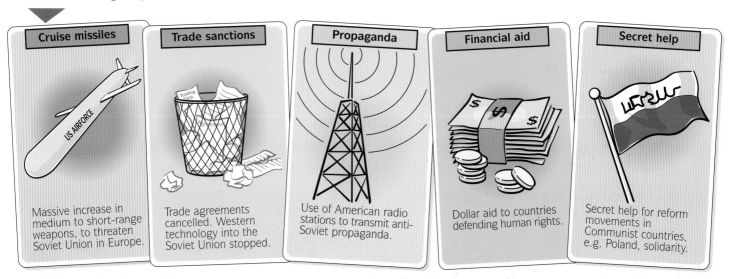

Cruise missiles	Trade sanctions	Propaganda	Financial aid	Secret help
Massive increase in medium to short-range weapons, to threaten Soviet Union in Europe.	Trade agreements cancelled. Western technology into the Soviet Union stopped.	Use of American radio stations to transmit anti-Soviet propaganda.	Dollar aid to countries defending human rights.	Secret help for reform movements in Communist countries, e.g. Poland, solidarity.

Europe: A nuclear battleground?

Many people in Western Europe feared the Soviet threat. By December 1979 there were over 600 Soviet SS-20 missiles in position.

Reagan decided to increase America's total defence spending, raising it from 178 billion dollars in 1981 to 367 billion in 1986.

The 108 Pershing II missiles and 464 ground-launched Cruise missiles (Source **E**) were small, and could be easily moved, so as to avoid detection. The Cruise missiles were low-flying, highly accurate, and so could evade detection by enemy radar. Cruise missiles eventually arrived in Europe in 1983.

The NATO decision to deploy Cruise missiles worsened East–West relations.

The fear of sudden attack by the Soviet Union led America to consider very expensive defence systems. In 1982 President Reagan decided that America would install the MX missile. This was a powerful long-range missile with many warheads, placed on underground tracks, which could be launched from different underground silos.

'Star Wars'

As expected, the 'Space Race' between the Great Powers had military links. The arms race was extended into space. By 1981 almost 2,000 military satellites had been launched. Both superpowers experimented with methods of destroying one another's missiles and satellites from space. America spent billions of dollars on laser and beam weapons designed to knock out Soviet long-range missiles (ICBMs) before they could reach their target.

In 1983, Reagan announced America's Strategic Defence Initiative (SDI) which was designed to build a protective laser shield around America against the possibility of Soviet missile attack. These weapons, based in space, gained the nickname of 'Star Wars'.

Source E A cruise missile in flight

Although vastly expensive, research was stepped up. In a test in January, 1984 America successfully destroyed a missile, in flight from space.

America's 'Star Wars' plan worried the Soviet Union. Despite the cost, the Soviet Union began its own programme of research into Star Wars. Before SDI, both Great Powers were equally vulnerable to nuclear missile attack. Now, if Soviet missiles could be destroyed before reaching their targets, then had American technology gained the upper hand in the arms race?

This new dimension to the arms race would be certain to make any future arms talks between the two Great Powers even more complicated and difficult.

Questions

1 Study Source **A**. What does it suggest about how President Reagan viewed Great Power relations?

2 How did Ronald Reagan use the situation in Afghanistan to set up another round in the Cold War against the Soviet Union?

Public reaction ... organised protest

 How did individuals protest against the arms race?
What was it like to live at Greenham Common as a peace protester?
How successful were the Greenham Common peace protesters?

How could ordinary citizens faced with nuclear annihilation, at 'the press of a button', make their voices heard?

Dissidents

Amongst the Communist Great Powers, military parades through Tianamen Square, Peking, and Red Square, Moscow were annual features (see front cover). The restrictive nature of the Soviet Union and China made organised public protest very difficult. Both Communist Super Powers attempted to restrict any individual dissidents who dared to criticise the state and its priorities. Nevertheless, brave individuals did protest about the growth of nuclear weapons and the effects of nuclear tests on the environment. Often, *dissidents* such as the Soviet Scientist Andrei Sakharov, and his wife Yelena Bonner, faced exile and imprisonment in remote parts of the Soviet Union.

CND

In Britain, various protest groups against war and nuclear weapons had existed – such as CND (the Campaign for Nuclear Disarmament) which was formed in 1958. Its traditional activity was a 50-mile march every Easter from London to an atomic weapons research site at Aldermaston.

As Great Power relations worsened in the 1980s, both superpowers looked to deploy new short and medium nuclear devices across the Iron Curtain in Europe. Source **A** suggests what many people in Western Europe feared.

Perhaps the Great Powers would prefer in the future to restrict a 'limited' nuclear to Europe? Already by 1979 there were over 600 SS-20 Soviet missiles ranged against targets in Western Europe. As soon as the Americans announced their plans to deploy 464 Cruise missiles on NATO bases a wave of anti-nuclear protests in Western Europe began. Demonstrations in West Germany topped the million mark. In Paris, 10,000 people formed a 'human chain'.

CND itself gained more members and increased its activities. As well as marches, mass 'die-ins' and huge demonstrations took place. In October 1983 a

Source A   Cartoon by Jim Borgman, 1982, showing Europe caught in the crossfire

CND rally attracted a crowd of 400,000 and brought central London to a standstill. On another occasion, demonstrators joined hands to link the Soviet and American Embassies in London.

Greenham Common

Greenham Common in Berkshire was one NATO base chosen to receive 96 American Cruise missiles in 1983.

From September 1982 onwards, the whole site was the scene of a remarkable 'embrace-the-base' round the clock vigil by thousands of peace-loving women. Liz Beech, herself a Greenham Common woman, reveals in Source **B** both her motivation and its effects on her family.

Source B
Liz Beech, recalling her 'Greenham days'

Obviously there were effects ... in leaving a family of four children. (I went) out of an entirely positive motive ... to rescue my children from the threat of nuclear holocaust ... I lost my own relationship ... my own marriage completely broke up during that period.

From *Woman's Hour*, BBC Radio 4, 1997

The Greenham Common women's main peace tactic was that of 'passive resistance' – in stark contrast to the deadly nuclear hardware about to be deployed. Instead of bombs, they made their protest by using the wire of the base to pin baby clothes, balloons and children's toys – which, to them, represented the future of the planet.

As time went by the Greenham Common women protesters received much publicity. Many people thought they were either stupid, naive or unpatriotic. Worse still, others thought they were pro-Communist. What cannot be denied is that the women were sincere in their beliefs and committed to their cause.

Once the Cruise missiles arrived on transporters, the women attempted to block the path of the missiles through to the base.

At times the women in the camps faced eviction by the authorities, as Jill Harding recalls in Source **E**.

Source E Jill Harding recalls her experiences of camp evictions

The experience of the Camp showed us how few things we could live with ... with the first few evictions they came along with the 'muncher' and threw everything into the back of it ... tents, blankets, sleeping bags ... we lost the lot. Gradually we came to cope with it ... and when they had gone, we would return the tents into their place.

From *Woman's Hour*, BBC Radio 4, 1997

Eventually the Cruise missiles arrived. The women stayed and attempted to disrupt the 'off-base' tactical deployments. In one sense, as Source **F** suggests, the women's campaign failed.

Source F The Greenham Common women's campaign

The Greenham Common women did not win. The Cruise Missiles stayed in Europe until they were withdrawn by the American government in 1989.

Extract from F. MacDonald and R. Staton, *The Cold War 1945–89*, Collins Educational, 1996

I lived at 'Orange Gate' ... I used to drive home in the morning, have a bath, get changed ... then go back to work ... I would come back in the evening, reverse the process, then go back to Camp ... Camp life was absolutely amazing.

From *Woman's Hour*, BBC Radio 4, 1997

Source C Jill Harding, by day a teacher, describes her 'double-life'

Source D British demonstrators trying to block the way to the cruise missile base at Greenham Common in the early 1980s

Yet today, at Greenham Common, where Cruise Missiles once stood, the former NATO base has been returned to common land and wild animals roam free.

Questions

1 How did protests against nuclear war differ in the Soviet Union compare to the West?

2 Study Source **A**. How does the cartoonist suggest:
   a) Great Power strength;
   b) Great Power attitudes to one another and to anti-nuclear protesters.

3 How effective were CND in achieving their aims and in shaping public opinion?

4 Which features made the demonstration at Greenham Common unique?

5 Study Source **D**. What is your opinion of such actions?

6 Source **F**, written in 1996, states that the Greenham Common women 'did not win'. Given what happened in 1989, do you agree with this view?

11 Steps towards ending the Cold War

Poland and 'Solidarity'

▶ **What part did 'Solidarity' play in bringing changes to Poland?**
How important was Lech Walesa to the process of reform?
What roles did the Great Powers play 'behind the scenes' in Poland?

Background

As the table opposite shows, everyday life in Poland was difficult by 1980.

'Solidarity'

Yet, within months, dramatic events happened. At the heart of the changes was a worker's organisation called 'Solidarity', shown in Source **A**, which was led by an electrician; Lech Walesa, shown in Source **B**.

Source A 'Solidarity' demonstration at a Gdansk shipyard in 1980

Poland by 1980	
Problem	**Situation**
Historical	Poland's recent past: German invasion, 1939. Soviet 'liberation' 1944/45. Soviet 'occupation' 1945.
Political	Since 1945 a Soviet 'satellite'. One-party state. Communist Government. Soviet Union disliked by millions of Polish citizens.
Religious	Eighty per cent of Poles members of Roman Catholic Church. Pope John Paul II Polish. Communist Government made religious worship difficult.
Economic	Food/fuel shortages. Goods in short supply. High prices.
Social: human rights	Free elections banned. Few workers. Benefits. Trade unions banned.

'Solidarity' began in protest against the high prices for fuel and food. Lech Walesa played a key role throughout. It was his leadership that persuaded the 17,000 workers at the Gdansk shipyards to go on strike for freedom and justice. Next he turned the workers' demands for higher wages into a campaign for 'Solidarity' to be allowed to exist as a free trade union; independent of the Communist Party.

As support for 'Solidarity' gathered strength, waves of strikes, marches and demonstrations crippled the northern coast of Poland. Although 'Solidarity's' members were all anti-Communist, they joined and supported democratisation for a variety of reasons.

Source B
Lech Walesa, making a speech to the members of 'Solidarity' in 1980

As 'Solidarity' grew, its members gained the support from some very important individuals living outside Poland.

72

- First, by the strength and independence of the Roman Catholic Church in Poland and the Polish people's loyalty to it.
- Secondly, through the covert intelligence operations of the American CIA. President Reagan saw the rise of 'Solidarity' as an ideal way to support an anti-Communist popular movement with modern technology and, thereby, try to undermine a key Communist satellite.
- Thirdly, through the indirect support for Polish Catholics, offered by the speeches and visit of Pope John Paul II.

- First, the Soviet Union felt stung by worldwide reaction to its invasion of Afghanistan.
- Secondly, America threatened the Soviet leaders that if they invaded Poland, America would sell weapons to China.

How would the authorities react? Earlier, Hungary (page 44) and Czechoslovakia (page 52) had been subject to 'the Brezhnev Doctrine': in the form of tank-backed Soviet 'crack downs'.

In Poland, after long and exhausting talks with the Government, 'Solidarity' was allowed to exist. It was the first independent trade union ever to be allowed to exist in a Soviet satellite. Why was such a change allowed to happen? The table above suggests two possible reasons for the Soviet response.

Next, 'Solidarity' demanded more say in political and economic changes. But, by 1981 Poland's economy faced ruin. Events took a turn for the worse. The Polish Army took over, under the 'hard-line' General Jaruzelski; under 'Emergency Powers', in 1982, 'Solidarity' was banned and even Lech Walesa was briefly imprisoned. The next year, 1983, Lech Walesa received recognition for his efforts to democratise Poland through the award of the 'Nobel Peace Prize'.

Source **C** shows another important moment, when the Pope, John Paul II, met Lech Walesa.

The Pope's visit attracted huge crowds. At Katowice, the Pope told the two million Poles assembled that people had a right to join free trade unions.

Source C   The Pope embraces Lech Walesa and his ideals

Source D
Extract from the Pope's sermon at Katowice, Poland, in June 1993

▶ This right is not given to us by the State. It is a right given to us by the Creator.

Although outlawed, 'Solidarity' continued to exist, and operate underground. This situation – though by no means ideal – was much better for the Poles than the alternative; a full-scale Soviet military invasion.

1 How important to 'Solidarity' was Lech Walesa?

2 Had Lech Walesa achieved his aims for Poland by 1993?

3 How important were the relative roles of these individuals:
   a) Ronald Reagan, and
   b) Pope John Paul II?

4 What part did the Pope play in the process of change in Poland?

5 How significant was the Pope's Polish nationality?

6 What part did the Roman Catholic Church play in bringing reforms to Poland?

7 Why was the CIA support for 'Solidarity' so important?

8 Why didn't the Soviet Union crush 'Solidarity' in Poland?

Questions

Mikhail Gorbachev

What impact did Mikhail Gorbachev's personality have upon Great Power relations? How did Gorbachev's policies ease external tensions and create internal opportunities?

After Brezhnev

In 1982, Premier Brezhnev died. The leadership fell next to two old men, Yuri Andropov – a former head of the KGB – and, soon after, Konstantin Chernenko. Both men were brought up through the Soviet Union's strict Stalin regime. They also shared a deep dislike and mistrust of America. As the Cold War worsened in the 1980s, Andropov walked out of arms talks taking place in Geneva. Chernenko was too ill to be an effective leader. Much of his work was undertaken by his deputy, Mikhail Gorbachev.

Personality

In appearance, style and manner, Gorbachev was completely different to the stereotype of Soviet leaders. He was young, aged 54, energetic, brisk, charming, intelligent, smiling and quick-witted with a warm sense of humour. In Raisa, a professional sociologist, he also had an equally intelligent and well-educated wife.

Through his friendliness and willingness to travel to the West to meet World leaders, Gorbachev created a favourable impression wherever he went; notably amongst the Americas when he met President Reagan in Geneva for informal talks in 1985.

Shortly after, he came to Britain and met the Prime Minister, Mrs Thatcher, who made the famous remark in Source **B**.

Problems

Upon taking power, as Source **C** suggests, Gorbachev faced many problems. Some were internal, and caused by Communism's inefficiency within the Soviet Union. Other problems were external, principally caused by the continuation of the Cold War with the West.

Gorbachev realised that major reforms to the internal policies of the Soviet Union were needed. In turn, for these to succeed then changes in the Soviet Union attitude towards the West and its commitments to satellites in Eastern Europe were necessary.

Source A Mikhail Gorbachev took over as Premier in 1985. What sort of person does he look like?

Source B
Margaret Thatcher

> He is a man who we can do business with.

Gorbachev's problems

Internal	External
Central planning – inefficient – corrupt.	High cost of arms race.
Industrial production falling.	High cost of controlling satellites in Eastern Europe.
Farming inefficient. Lack of food.	Cost of maintaining Afghanistan war: no victory in sight.
Shortages of goods.	
Inflation.	

'Perestroika' and 'Glasnost'

In 1986 Gorbachev attacked Brezhnev for 'years of stagnation'.

Gorbachev, a life-long Communist, believed in its ideology and hoped to revive the Soviet Union's economy by improving its output, market and technology.

He decided to tackle the nation's problems by introducing two linked policies shown in the table below designed to improve life in the Soviet Union.

'Perestroika' and 'Glasnost'

'Perestroika' (Re-structuring)	'Glasnost' (Openness)
The Soviet State should be re-built: ● to stamp out corruption ● to provide goods people wanted at a price they cost to make ● to remove the central planning by the Government in economics ● for everyone to do their job properly.	The Soviet Union and its citizens should: ● be more democratic ● have more freedom from Government control ● have more freedom of speech ● have more media freedom ● have leaders who should listen to people's views and accept criticism.

Within the Soviet Union, Gorbachev's policies were received with confusion and he became unpopular. Some citizens resented the changes and refused to accept them. Others complained about the slow pace of change. Elsewhere in the Soviet Union the idea of 'Glasnost' led to a growing demand for greater independence amongst some powerful republics.

Source C Ronald Reagan speaking in Geneva, 21 November 1985

The two powers can make a fresh start ... I can not claim we had a meeting of minds and such fundamentals as ideology or nation purpose, but we understand each other better.

'Gorby mania'

In stark contrast, wherever Gorbachev travelled abroad he was mobbed as the most charming and approachable leader that the Soviet Union ever had.

For his attempts to limit the arms race (see page 76) and his policies towards Eastern Europe (see page 78) he received honours from the West such as the 'Nobel Peace Prize' and the 'Man of the Year'.

Despite the shadow of the Cold War, personal relations between President Reagan and Premier Gorbachev warmed, as Sources **C** and **D** both suggest.

How would Gorbachev's bold ideas to reduce the costs of competing in the arms race, and in supporting its Eastern European satellites be put into place? Could Gorbachev control the forces that he might unleash?

Source D Mikhail Gorbachev speaking on Geneva on 21 November, 1985

The World has become a safer place ... (he was) ... very optimistic.

Questions

1 Why was Gorbachev's personality such an asset to him?

2 Explain how Gorbachev's twin policies, shown in the table above, were designed to address the Soviet Union's problems.

3 How were the prospects of 'perestroika's success linked to those of 'glasnost'?

4 Why did the ideas behind 'glasnost' lead to a varied response in the Soviet Union?

5 How might the peoples of Eastern Europe view the prospects of 'glasnost?

Summits and arms treaties

> **What reasons lay behind the Great Power motives to reduce nuclear weapons? Which Great Power leader – Reagan or Gorbachev – deserves most credit for reducing the threat of nuclear war?**

New opportunities

The arrival of Premier Gorbachev, and his attitude towards the West, offered new opportunities for improved relations with America. Within four short years major changes happened. The result was a series of summit meetings and arms treaties, mostly concerned with reducing the number of nuclear weapons held by each Great Power.

Great Power motives

What caused such a major shift in Great Power thinking? For both Great Powers the cost of the arms race was enormous. The Soviet Union spent 25% of the country's wealth on arms spending, its defence budget was totally out of control. Mikhail Gorbachev's attitudes were based on several linked intentions, shown in the table opposite.

Even President Reagan whose 'tough-talking' against Communism got him re-elected and made him one of America's most popular presidents, realised that the cost of the arms race was considerable.

Summits and the INF

How would the leaders grasp this chance for arms reductions? After initial meetings of diplomats, the two leaders met face to face at Reykjavik in Iceland in 1986. Though 'Star Wars' was a sticking point, later meetings were arranged. At their next meeting, in Washington 1987, a significant step was taken. The two Great Power leaders signed an Intermediate-range Nuclear Forces (INF) Treaty (Source **A**).

In June 1988 this was *ratified* in Moscow when President Reagan visited the Soviet Union. Was this the beginning of the end of the Cold War?

Effects

The effects of the INF treaty were scenes that had not previously been dreamt of. In America and Western

---

Premier Gorbachev's motives

- He wanted peace between East and West, along the earlier lines of 'peaceful co-existence'.
- He wanted to end the expensive and dangerous arms race.
- In 1986 he proposed a fifteen year scheme to rid the world of nuclear weapons by AD 2000.
- He was concerned about Reagan's 'Star Wars' scheme.
- He realised that despite Soviet attempts to respond, it didn't have either the budget – or technology – to compete.
- He realised that the Soviet Union needed to spend much less on arms and far more on improvements at home.

Source A   President Reagan and Premier Gorbachev signing the first nuclear arms agreement

Europe, Pershing Missiles were destroyed and Cruise missiles were withdrawn (see page 85). Work on 'Star Wars' research was halted. In the Soviet Union and Eastern Europe, SS-20 missiles were withdrawn, and – as in Source **B** – destroyed, and bombers were dismantled.

Source B Soviet SS-20 missiles being destroyed at Kaspoutin Yar Base, 1988

In December 1989, the two most powerful men in the world met on board a storm-tossed warship. The purpose of their meeting was truly historic. They had met to agree to end the Cold War.

From F. Macdonald and R. Staton, *The Cold War*, Collins 1996

Importantly, each Great Power was able to check that the other was carrying out the agreed arms reductions.

Source C The meeting between Gorbachev and Bush

'The Cold War is Over'

The genuine moves to disarmament, together with Gorbachev's attitudes to events in Eastern Europe (pages 78–79) resulted in one final summit whose objective is outlined in Source **C**.

Mikhail Gorbachev met America's new President, George Bush, to hail a new era in Superpower relations Source **D** suggests how George Bush saw the Summit.

The two leaders outlined plans to sign two arms control pacts, one to half strategic nuclear weapons, the other to reduce conventional forces in Europe.

After a series of friendly meetings, the two leaders officially declared that the Cold War was over.

Not so long ago, some believed that the weight of history condemned our two great countries, our two great peoples, to permanent confrontation. Well, you and I must challenge history, make new strides, build a relationship of enduring co-operation'.

We may not agree on everything, but we believe in one great truth: the world has waited long enough, the Cold War must end.'

Source D President Bush speaking at the Malta Summit, December 1989

Questions

1 Why was it so important for the Soviet Union to reduce its arms spending?

2 How much credit does Premier Gorbachev deserve for ending the Cold War?

3 How helpful were the American Presidents Reagan and Bush in promoting arms cuts?

4 Look back to earlier sections on Protect … survive … protest (page 33) and Afghanistan (page 66). How might these people feel about the following events:

a) a Greenham Common woman – when Cruise missiles left the base in 1989, and
b) a Mujahaddin rebel – when the last Soviet soldier left in 1989?

5 Study Source **B**. How would the following feel upon witnessing the scenes:
a) a Soviet missile technician, and
b) a Soviet Air Force pilot?

6 How far did Gorbachev's policy of 'perestroika' depend on significant arms reductions?

Glasnost spreads: Poland and Eastern Europe

▶ **Did 'Glasnost' also apply to the Soviet Union's satellites in Eastern Europe?**
What might some of the effects be upon the countries concerned?
How might the Soviet Union respond to any attempts to change Eastern Europe?

Introduction

How would the millions of people living in the Soviet satellite states in Eastern Europe react to Gorbachev's ideas? To them all thoughts of 'Glasnost' seemed a stark contrast to the strict 'hard-line' Communist govern-ments installed in the ancient capitals of Eastern Europe. Images of the 'Brezhnev Doctrine' i.e. Soviet tanks 'restoring order' (in 1956 and 1968) lived long in people's memories.

Yet now, under Gorbachev and Glasnost, how might the Soviet Union react to any popular protest?

The 'Sinatra Doctrine'

Gorbachev realised that the Soviet Union could not afford to 'prop up' Communist regimes in Eastern Europe. In 1986 he announced that Soviet tanks would no longer appear to support any Communist governments facing trouble. Nor would leaders be told what to do by telephone from Moscow. Instead, Gorbachev believed that people should be allowed to choose their own form of government and go their own way. This policy became known as the 'Sinatra Doctrine' after the Frank Sinatra song 'My Way'. Whether Gorbachev expected all the incredible events which his policy unleashed, with such speed, is unknown.

Poland
(see table opposite)

Source A
The Sinatra Doctrine

East Germany
1989
• Change of leader
• Mass street protests

Czechoslovakia
1989
• Demonstrations
• Resignation of Communists
• Non-Communist President
• Democratic elections

Romania
• The most brutal government in Eastern Europe

Hungary
1988
• Demonstrations
1990
• Democratic elections

Bulgaria
1990
• Elections but Communists re-elected

0   km   300

Poland: 'Solidarity' returns

With its economy once again in ruins, under martial law, led by an unpopular hard-line military Communist in General Jaruzelski and its peoples' favoured protest group – 'Solidarity' - banned Poland was in dire straits. Despite this, as Source **B** shows, it did have the potential for reform.

- 'Solidarity' though illegal, went 'underground'.
- Helped by American spy organisations and aid, it distributed leaflets, newspapers to workers.
- 'Solidarity' suggested that workers adopt 'passive resistance' against the authorities attempts to set Poland's economy straight.
- The Catholic Church in Poland was very popular. It offered millions of Poles a powerful alternative to believe in.
- The Pope played a big part. He suggested that if General Jaruzelski introduced reforms – then he would visit Poland.
- Gorbachev's policy of Glasnost offered workers a chance to re-create 'Solidarity' and remove the Communist government.

Source B   A red star is taken down in Budapest, Hungary, in October 1989

By 1988 waves of unofficial protest strikes swept across Poland. Once again, Lech Walesa had talks with the government. 'Solidarity' was made legal, strikes were allowed and, most importantly, free elections were promised. These were the first ones ever allowed in any Communist country. Solidarity was able to contrast the election and won all the available seats open to non-Communists. Despite not having popular support the Communists stayed in power, but in July 1989, Jaruzelski was forced to appoint a non-Communist Roman Catholic to be Poland's prime minister. Poland had set a trend – different parties, non-Communist governments, trade unions and prime ministers. The 'icing' on the long-suffering Pole's 'cake' came in 1990 when Lech Walesa was elected as President of Poland.

'Glasnost' spreads

Events in other satellites, such as Hungary and Czechoslovakia followed very similar paths. Large numbers of people would take to the streets demanding changes.

Rather than suppress the demonstrators the Soviet Union would stand back and allow events to take their course. Sometimes the Communist governments simply resigned as in Czechoslovakia, allowing non-Communist parties and presidents to become elected after democratic elections.

Elsewhere, as Source **B** shows, Hungary all-party elections ousted the Communist Party from power.

The spirit of 'Glasnost' led to other historic events. The back cover shows border guards from Hungary cutting through the Iron Curtain! This highly symbolic act led to various effects:

- An 'exit point' for many refugees – mostly fleeing from East Germany – was created. An exodus of refugees fled to the West throughout 1989.

- By ignoring 'Glasnost' East Germany became isolated, as it became surrounded by new democracies. Its leader, Erich Honecker, forced millions of East Germans to live under his dictatorship. Official propaganda, censorship and police informers were everywhere.
- Despite its secure borders of wire and wall, ordinary East Germans demanded more freedom. As always, East Germany's leaders looked to Moscow for advice, but under 'glasnost' what might the answer be?

For a time, some hard-line satellites like Bulgaria, East Germany and Romania stayed loyal to the Soviet Union. Their leaders were desperate to cling to power, despite the rising tide of public opinion.

Yet, within weeks, even more dramatic events would sweep them all from power and with them all other visible traces of Communism.

1 Explain, simply, what the Soviet Union meant by the 'Sinatra Doctrine'.

2 How significant were the roles of these individuals to the events in Poland:
   a) Lech Walesa;
   b) Pope John Paul II.

3 Were Gorbachev's motives to allow 'Glasnost' in the satellites based upon:
   a) a desire to set Eastern Europe 'free';
   b) a wish to allow Communism to restructure those countries;
   c) a desire to save money, so that more could be spent on re-building the Soviet Union.

4 Do you think Mikhail Gorbachev expected his policy to lead to the breakdown of Communism across Eastern Europe?

5 How important were Hungary's actions in helping create the mass exodus to the West?

Questions

12 Towards a new world order

Communism crumbles: the Berlin Wall

How did the Berlin Wall's destruction come about?
How did ordinary people caught up in events, react to
the era of Communism in East Germany?

Concrete and changes

Have you ever visited the Imperial War Museum in
London? Among all the tanks and aircraft is an
unusual exhibit, shown in Source **A**.

Source **B** shows an earlier stage in its eventful life.

Source A
A segment of
the Berlin
Wall

Source B   Delighted Germans take the Berlin Wall apart

What happened in Berlin to bring about such an
important change?

Tensions rise

By autumn 1989 those still forced to live in East
Germany were at boiling point. For four decades they
had been denied access to, or information about, the
West. East Germany was like a powder keg.

Gorbachev told East Germany's leaders to make
'fundamental reforms' and to listen to the 'impulses'
of the times. His advice was ignored; no changes
would be made. But, with the iron curtain opened

in Hungary, thousands of East Germans had already
fled westwards (see page 79). To try to settle a tense
situation the Party switched its leader. Honecker
resigned and Egon Krenz took over. His ideas for
reform failed to impress. Millions took to the streets
in Leipzig and in East Berlin.

- Why should they have to uproot, and become a
  refugee, in the West?
- Why couldn't they travel to and from the West as
  free citizens?
- Why did they have to be trapped inside their own
  country, like prisoners, by the Berlin Wall?

'Borders will be opened'

November 9 1989. A day of confusion. Two Berliners – Harold Jager, a border guard, and Barbel Reinke – both sit down to watch the TV news. At a live press conference a Party official states that 'all borders will be opened'.

> Gorbachev was our one great hope. Someone in my street sprayed 'Gorbachev' on the Wall. We had such hopes of him.
>
> From *The People's Century*, BBC, 1997

Source C Barbel Reinke, a waitress in Berlin, recalled how many felt about a visit about to be made by Premier Gorbachev

Source D Harold Jager recalls his reaction

> He turned his paper and said 'immediately', I thought that's impossible – he's talking nonsense.
>
> From *The People's Century*, BBC, 1997

Barbel Reinke's reaction, like thousands of others, differed. Immediately she set off for the Berlin Wall, intending to walk through the West. Upon arriving, a shock awaited her. Across the Brandenburg Gate – as always – stood a line of armed border guards. Barbel's pleading to be allowed through was filmed by a TV news crew (Source **E**).

> I beg you ... who's in charge here? ... we've been waiting so long ... I cannot take any more ... Once in my life I want to walk through the Brandenburg Gate ... I just want to see the other side ...

Source E Barbel Reinke's comments to border guards, from a TV news report, 9 November 1997

The Wall comes down

At the stroke of midnight Barbel was allowed through. Thousands passed through the checkpoints, many climbed over the Wall itself. Scenes of wild delight followed. In following days some people took pick axes and hammers to the Wall, as Source **B** shows, determined to help destroy the ugly symbol of East–West divide.

The opening of the Berlin Wall, led to outpourings of joy in the capitals of the West. President Bush was 'elated'. Even the Soviet Union saw that the end of the Berlin Wall was 'symbolic'. Millions of Germans looked forward to a new future. This was especially so after October 1990, when the two separate Germanies, East and West, became re-united as one nation again.

Postscript

One German not looking forward to the next few years is Egon Krenz. Source **F** reveals his fate, which was decided in 1997.

> ### LAST RED JAILED FOR KILLINGS AT WALL
>
> Final bid to bring East German Communist leadership to book

Source F Newspaper headline from the *Independent*.

Questions

1 a) Does Source **A** deserve its place as an exhibit in a museum about war in the twentieth century?
b) Explain why only one side of the Wall shows signs of graffiti. Use Source **B** to help you.
c) A slab of Berlin Wall has recently arrived at the museum. The curator has asked you to write an information panel to go on display next to the exhibit. Write out a draft of your ideas.

2 a) Was it fair for Egon Krenz in Source **F** to be given a six and a half year jail sentence?
b) What do you think of his defence 'that he was only carrying out orders from Moscow'?

3 Why was the opening of the Wall such a symbolic act?

4 What might Barbel Reinke and Harold Jager each think about:
a) the destruction of the Wall in 1990?
b) the creation of a single Germany in 1990?
c) the jailing of Egon Krenz in 1997?

The break-up of the Soviet Union

▶ Why did Communism collapse in the Soviet Union?
What replaced the Communist Party?
What was Gorbachev's fate?

When Soviet cosmonaut Sergei Krikalev blasted off into space in July 1991 he expected to return, five months later, to the Soviet Union the way it was when he left it (see Source **B**).

Source A
Cosmonaut Sergei Krikalev returns to earth, 26 March 1992

Source B The Soviet Union under Communism, 1917–91

Upon his return, shown in Source **A**, several surprises awaited him, as the newpaper report in Source **C** explains.

Source C Helen Womak in Moscow, from the *Independent*, 26 March 1992

Whilst he was otherwise engaged, the Communist utopia failed on Earth, his old country ceased to exist, his home town of Leningrad was renamed St Petersburg and the Soviet space programme collapsed ... He was told about last August's failed coup, the banning of the Communist Party, Mikhail Gorbachev's resignation and the fall of the Soviet Union.

There's no food, no cars, nothing in the shops. What's the point in having money when there is nothing to buy? I've come to hate Gorbachev ... I hate the bloody Communists as well. They've wrecked this country.

This view was, I found, entirely representative ... No one had a good word to say for the Communist Party or Gorbachev.

The remarkable changes in Source **C** can be traced back to Gorbachev's twin policies of perestroika and glasnost. His own fate though was ironic, although he was vastly popular overseas this wasn't the case at home. John Simpson, for the BBC, observed the mood in Leningrad in 1990 (see Source **D**).

By opening up the debate on how to improve the standards of living within the Soviet Union, Gorbachev brought about his own downfall. In 1991, the public eventually lost patience with the speed of his reforms. His harshest critic was Boris Yeltsin, the

Source D John Simpson, BBC TV News Report, April 1990

President of Russia, the largest and strongest of the Soviet Union's 15 republics. In allowing the possibilities of open elections and a multi-party state, Gorbachev released unstoppable forces of nationalism which led to independence and the break up of the republics which previously made up the Soviet Union. Source **E** shows the self-governing republics which emerged by 1992.

Source E Independent republics of the Russian Federation

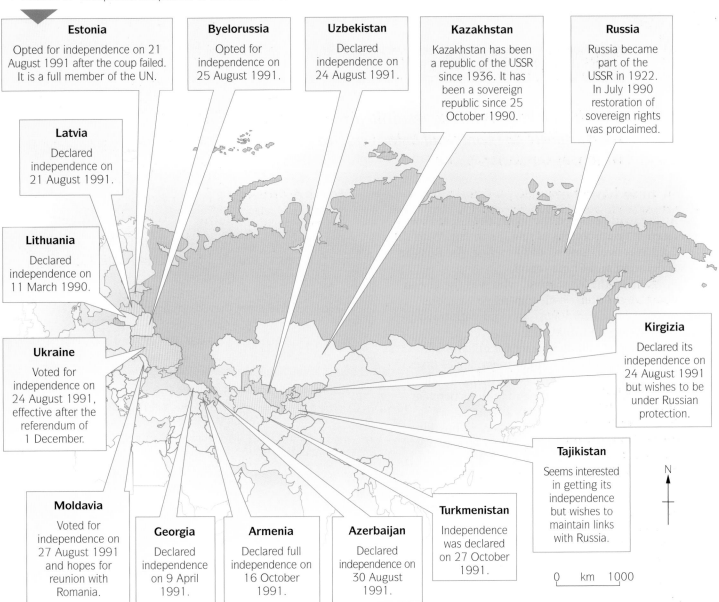

Estonia
Opted for independence on 21 August 1991 after the coup failed. It is a full member of the UN.

Byelorussia
Opted for independence on 25 August 1991.

Uzbekistan
Declared independence on 24 August 1991.

Kazakhstan
Kazakhstan has been a republic of the USSR since 1936. It has been a sovereign republic since 25 October 1990.

Russia
Russia became part of the USSR in 1922. In July 1990 restoration of sovereign rights was proclaimed.

Latvia
Declared independence on 21 August 1991.

Lithuania
Declared independence on 11 March 1990.

Kirgizia
Declared its independence on 24 August 1991 but wishes to be under Russian protection.

Ukraine
Voted for independence on 24 August 1991, effective after the referendum of 1 December.

Tajikistan
Seems interested in getting its independence but wishes to maintain links with Russia.

Moldavia
Voted for independence on 27 August 1991 and hopes for reunion with Romania.

Georgia
Declared independence on 9 April 1991.

Armenia
Declared full independence on 16 October 1991.

Azerbaijan
Declared independence on 30 August 1991.

Turkmenistan
Independence was declared on 27 October 1991.

N

0   km   1000

Once independent, many republics turned their back on Communism and its ideas. Many long established symbols of Soviet power were removed. Once stripped of power, and forced to resign, Gorbachev reflected upon his fate (see Source **F**).

Source F Resignation speech by Mikail Gorbachev, Soviet TV, December 1991

The old system fell apart before the new one began to work

Questions

1 Gorbachev's fate was ironic. The historian Eric Hobsbawm wrote in 1994 that, 'he was a tragic figure who destroyed what he wanted to reform, and was himself destroyed in the process.' How far was Gorbachev at fault for the end of Communist rule in the Soviet Union?

2 Why did Gorbachev become so unpopular in the Soviet Union?

3 Which of Gorbachev's policies led to a wish to break away from Communism?

4 How do you think Ronald Reagan would view the break-up of the 'Evil Empire'?

5 Some regard Gorbachev as a hero of the twentieth century; others see him as a failure. What is your own opinion?

The peace dividend

> **Did the end of the Cold War result in a more peaceful world?**
> **Did the 'peace dividend' lead to the expected higher standards of living?**

'A new world order'

As the world entered the 1990s the Great Powers faced major problems of re-adjustment. With the Cold War over, how would America, the Russian Federation and China react?

As far as the West went, who was the enemy now? Might their vastly expensive weapons systems be scaled down – or even withdrawn – from Western Europe?

There was talk of a 'peace for all' and of a 'peace dividend'. This might mean lower taxes, leading to a higher standard of living for all, because of less need to spend billions per year on expensive military forces and arms.

Despite four decades of East–West hostility, many people held out the hope of a 'new world order'.

Russia's response

Source **A** shows that the Russian Federation did try to reduce its arms.

Abroad Russia became much more accepted on the World stage. For instance, Yeltsin regularly travelled to the 'G7' meetings held by the key World leaders to discuss matters of trade and commerce.

America in particular saw Yeltsin as a strong and stable leader and supported him whenever possible.

Source A   Missile being dismantled

I'm Leonid Shukov. I've worked here for 12 years. Tell me this, why are we disarming?
The way I see it, things are more unstable now than they were under the Communists …

Look, we're still surrounded, as ever, by America. China is a growing threat. We've no satellites anymore. The Warsaw Pact's been wound up. Gorbachev's thrown away our buffer zone … and Germany's already reunited itself …

… and what about the nuclear missiles scattered all over the Federation? What if some of the new Republics flex their nuclear muscles? At least in the old days, under the Party, all our forces were under one unified command, but now … Anyway, are the American's disarming?… Can we be sure? …

America's response

Source **B** shows graphic evidence that, at one famous NATO base – Greenham Common – not only had the Cruise missiles been withdrawn, but the wire was coming down, with the whole of the site being returned to nature.

Source B Photograph showing Greenham Common wire removal

> I'm a spokesperson for CND. The final removal of the fences at Greenham Common and its return to common land is a day for celebrating and a testimony to the hundreds of thousands of peace campaigners. For 14 years, the Greenham Women have been an inspiration to people around the World for their energy, determination and focus.
>
> The CND now looks forwards to the day when all the fences come down at all nuclear bases and installations.

The cuts in American defence spending also failed to deliver a 'peace dividend'. Although many Americans have a very high standard of living, not all share in their country's wealth.

As both America and the Russian Federation grappled with their internal problems, neither saw the wider picture. The gap between the rich world and poor world continues to grow. The end of the Cold War has failed to end either war or widespread poverty. Worse still, both Great Powers are key suppliers of arms, training and advice to many nations around the world.

Questions

1 How might these individuals regard the 'peace dividend':
   a) Leonid Shukov, in Source **A**?
   b) The spokesperson for CND in Source **B**?

2 Why has America been so keen to support Boris Yeltsin in power?

3 Has the end of the Cold War made the world:
   a) a safer place?
   b) a more peaceful place?

4 Have the Great Powers used the end of the Cold War wisely? What is your own view about:
   a) the 'peace dividend';
   b) the 'new world order'.

13 An unstable world

China: Tianamen ... triumph to tears

▶ **What were Mao and Deng's policies for modernising China?**
Which movement lived – and died – in 1989?
Which future issues face China?

China under Mao

Under Mao, Communist China was kept in a state of 'continuous revolution' – in terms of key areas of farming, industry, education, health, culture and women's roles. Some policies failed, others succeeded. Such internal instability worried the Soviet Union, which led – in time – to the Sino-Soviet split (see page 56). Mao's attitude to America and its capitalist ideology was largely hostile.

China under Deng

Mao died in 1976. China's new leader, Deng Xiaoping, wished to modernise China as the table opposite shows.

Tianamen, 1989

By 1989, with Gorbachev in power – due to visit China, and with 'Glasnost' in the air, might the time be right for some political changes in China? Many students, supported by *dissidents* and some workers, protested for greater democracy in China.

What followed – between April and June 1989 – is captured below in a graphic sequence of photographs which the world viewed with horror.

Triumph ...

Deng's priorities in China	
'The four modernisations'	
● Agriculture ● Industry	More freedom to grow, sell and retain profits. Small, private businesses allowed.
● Science ● Defence	Emphasis on technology, including modern nuclear weapons, see front cover.
'The one child policy'	
● Population control	One child per married couple – rewards, punishments.
● A willingness to allow Western businesses, trade and tastes into China.	Increase in trade. Sixty American firms set up in China.

Source A Tianamen Square protesters, April 1989

... Tears

After Tianamen, which Deng brushed off as 'an incident' *Martial Law* was declared. Many hundreds of students were rounded up, arrested and put on trial as 'traitors to the people'.

Source B A victim of the Tianamen Square massacre

Source C The night after the Tianamen Square massacre a young man stepped in front of a moving column of tanks, forcing them to stop

After Deng

Deng Xiaoping died, aged 92, in 1997. Since 1949, China has only had two Communist leaders, first Mao then Deng.

Deng in particular helped guide China's path from a nation made up of millions of illiterate peasants into a modern and forward-looking Great Power.

Looking ahead, two major questions will be, who will emerge to lead China, and more interestingly, how will the only surviving Communist Great Power fare in the twenty-first century?

Questions

1 What might Mao think of Deng's priorities for China (see table on page 86)?

2 **a)** Which of the sources, **A–C** has the most impact upon you?
   b) Select the source of your choice.
      i) Explain why you've chosen it.
      ii) How does it explain the events at Tianamen in 1989?
   c) How could the protesters use it as publicity for their cause?
   d) How could the authorities use it as a source of propaganda against the protesters?

3 Which major issues face China in the twenty-first century?

Difficulties of democratisation

▶ **How well has the Russian Federation coped with the new ideas of capitalism and democracy?**
What problems have arisen by 'mothballing' the Federation's armed forces?

Coping with capitalism

With the break-up of the Soviet Union and the end of Communism, millions of citizens found themselves living under new political and economic systems.

Under perestroika, Mikhail Gorbachev did try to introduce Western ideas of profit making, partly by inviting major American businesses to set up, such as McDonalds.

For many people, the idea the Communist Party would no longer plan everything was hard to grasp. No one had any experience of capitalism. Many people abused the system and created the series of linked problems shown in the table opposite.

Problems for the Russian Federation
● Widespread corruption.
● Absenteeism.
● Drug abuse.
● Widespread organised crime.
● Poverty.
● Food shortages.
● Consumer goods shortages.
● Fierce nationalism in many republics.
● Leading, at worst, to civil war.
● Armed intervention by Russian troops.

Yeltsin's aims

Boris Yeltsin inherited these problems. He would agree with the idea in Source **A**.

Source A An extract from a letter to a Soviet newspaper

The World has moved on. The Party didn't make good use of its seventy-two years.

As well as holding the new Russian Federation together, Yeltsin set himself the two aims shown below.

Yeltsin's aims
● To introduce a Western-style *market-style* economy.
● To introduce democracy into the newly independent republics.

Source B A newspaper extract, via Reuters News Agency, from the *Independent*, 1996

Moscow (Reuters) – A strike by hungry workers at a nuclear shipyard in the town of Severodvinsk near the northern port of Arkhangelsk could escalate into a riot unless they are quickly paid long overdue wages, a local union leader has warned. He said there had been cases of workers fainting from hunger and a number of suicides.

Source C Russian nuclear submarines

Problems ... problems ...

Given Russia's problems, it is hardly surprising that Yeltsin faced difficulties. Yet, as Sources **B**, **C** and **D** indicate, the end of the Cold War created a range of new problems. How far might these have been predicted by Russia's leaders?

Source D Martin Sixmith, a BBC TV Foreign Correspondent, presented the following news item in November 1996

Mothballed and neglected, Russia's front-line is now used mainly for hanging out the washing. In the port of Baltisk, 80 warships have been laid up for more than a year. With no fuel to go to sea they are increasingly being handed over to the homeless families of Officers and Ratings that the navy can no longer afford to house.

Source E The son of a Russian sailor who lives aboard a moth-balled warship

At first it was all a bit of an adventure but now we're all fed up with it. The problem is that our footballs keep going over the side. There's just nowhere for us to play.

Source F Captain Valery Udovichenko on the BBC news, 12 November 1996

I used to love the Navy and doing the work. I want to serve, but when I see my ship in such a dire position, well, what can I say? No one here has been paid since August.

They feel abandoned and hardly in a mood to fight for their country. For months there hasn't even been enough to eat … there's always the nettles, there's plenty of them to eat … in fact eating nettles is what the pride of the Russian navy has been reduced to – a diet that has soured the morale of this unhappy fleet and highlighted the military disintegration that's fast becoming Boris Yeltsin's biggest headache.

From a report by Martin Sixmith

Nationalism

A second thorn in Yeltsin's side has been extreme nationalism and how best to deal with it. At times his decisions seemed at odds with his aim to democratise the Federation. Chechynya, which declared its independence in 1994, offers a classic example (see Source **E**, page 83). Without consulting Parliament, Yeltsin ordered Russian tanks in to remove the Chechynya leader. His idea of a swift victory backfired. Against overwhelming odds, the Chechynyans fought off the Russian army for over two years.

Despite losing between 20,000 and 100,000 people, over 4,000 Russian troops also died. Eventually, the Russian troops – humiliated by such a small force of rebels – left, without disarming them.

A new problem

This episode showed Yeltsin's ruthless streak, and did little for his image as a protector of human rights. With this in mind there was a certain irony that when Boris Yeltsin met President Clinton for a summit meeting in March 1997 in Helsinki. The very place where, 22 years earlier, the high point of détente was reached (see page 63). This time though the key agenda wasn't human rights. Instead, as Source **E** reveals, with the collapse of the Warsaw Pact, something totally new was on the agenda!

NATO EXPANSION AT UNEASY HEART OF US–RUSSIA TALKS

Source G Newspaper headline from *The Times*, 21 March 1997

Questions

1 Use a copy of Source **B** to undertake a DARTS exercise.
   a) Underline, with a highlighter, the problems outlined in the source.
   b) Which of the problems that you've found:
     i) were a direct result of the break-up of Communism?
     ii) were a direct result of the 'peace dividend'?

2 How many of the problems you have identified could have been predicted by Russia's leaders?

3 Use the ideas you've gathered – along with other information – to explain the difficulties that Boris Yeltsin faced in modernising the Russian Federation.

Problems of realignment

 **What problems have the planned expansion of NATO led to?
How has this issue been interpreted in different ways?**

The East looks to the West

● in trade and business – by 'sounding out' Western Europe to see if membership of the European Community (EC) was open to them;

● by strengthening their defence and security by making a formal application to join NATO; the West's foremost military alliance.

With the old certainties of the Cold War ended, millions of East Europeans in former Soviet 'buffer-zone' countries searched for new opportunities. Those in Poland were typical. Even after hard-line Communism ended and 'Solidarity' gained control (see page 72), by 1993 something like 70% of the population were unhappy with democracy. With such severe problems, introducing any reforms was hard and making capitalist ideas work was difficult. As a result, in the 1990s, countries like Poland have been run by different governments.

Like several other nations, the newly democratic, capitalist Poland looked to the West for help in the two key directions shown in the table above.

Source **A** offers a clear view of Boris Yeltsin's attitude towards the plans to expand NATO. He was, and is, totally against the idea. The key 'sticking point' for Yeltsin was the possible deployment of NATO nuclear weapons in Poland, Hungary and the Czech Republic.

As Source **B** suggests, the age-old fear of 'encirclement' and linked threats of invasion have returned.

Source A Dutch cartoon, showing NATO tempting Eastern Europe from Mother Russia, by Behrendt

The Americans hoped that the Russian Federation might be a willing partner to the NATO expansion document. It was not to be. Feelings in 'Mother Russia' ran deep, as Source **C** reveals.

Source B 'Fear of Encirclement', from the *Independent*, 1997

We fear that as it gains strength and moves closer to Russian borders, NATO will try to impose on us its conditions – political, economic and others.

Source C Comment by Russia Defence Minister, General Igor Rodionov, in the *Guardian*, 20 February 1997

Fear of encirclement: How the Russians see the world

RUSSIA

USA
NATO
CHECHNYA
IRAN
AFGHANISTAN
CHINA
NUCLEAR WEAPONS (12,000)
BANK STATEMENT

Current NATO countries

Whatever Russia's objections, as the Madrid Summit approached five former Communist countries in Eastern Europe hoped their application to join NATO would succeed. But as Western political and military leaders met, Boris Yeltsin refused to attend.

Source D Newspaper extract from the *Independent*, 9 July 1997

Nato Secretary-General announced the historic decision to invite Poland, Hungary and the Czech republic to join. The announcement signals the biggest single expansion in Nato's 48-year history and is the first to embrace countries which not long ago faced the 16-nation Western Alliance in armed confrontation.

Source **D** reveals the outcome of the Madrid Summit. It pleased three nations, disappointed two – Romania and Slovenia – and angered one. The Russian Foreign Minister showed his anger in Source **E**.

Source E Russian Foreign Minister Yevgeny Primakov, speaking in Moscow, from the *Independent*, 9 July 1997

We still consider expansion the biggest mistake in Europe since the end of the Second World War.

Source F C. Bellamy and E. Nash, in Madrid for the NATO summit, from the *Independent*, 9 July 1997

NATO won the Cold War

NATO, for its part, having gained 3,082,000 more armed forces and 14% more territory opened the door for future invitations for membership.

Interpretations about NATO's expansion in the British press were mixed. What follows are newspaper extracts offering different interpretations of the same event.

NATO EMBRACES EASTERN PARTNERS IN BIGGEST STEP FOR HALF A CENTURY

Invitation to Poles, Hungarians and Czechs was expected, but still infuriates Russia

The first three states from the former Soviet bloc have been invited to join the Nato military alliance in 1999

The alliance has comprehensively won the Great Cold War confrontation for which it was created without firing a shot.

Take expansion ... these first new admissions are taking place for the most basic of Cold War reasons: fear of Russia. Poland, the Czech Republic and Hungary admit quite openly that they are seeking membership to ensure protection from their giant neighbour to the East.

Source G Extract from leading article in the *Independent*, 9 July 1997

Questions

1 Study Source **A**.
a) Why has the cartoonist drawn the figures representing NATO, East Europe and Yeltsin in the ways shown?
b) What 'image' of NATO membership is being offered to Eastern Europe?
c) What 'image' of ignoring NATO's advances is shown?
d) How does the cartoonist convey ideas of age, attractiveness and power as far as East Europe is concerned?

2 Study Source **B**. Do you think Boris Yeltsin's fears seem justified?

3 Compare Source **B**, drawn in 1997, with earlier sources showing encirclement (page 6, page 39).
a) What are the similarities?
b) What are the differences?

4 Why do you think Poland, Hungary and the Czech Republic wanted to join NATO?

5 Consider how you would organise – and pitch – a brief, one minute, Radio News Report on the outcome of the NATO Madrid Summit. Think about your audience, what they might wish to hear, your own opinion and any historical parallels, etc.

6 Do you agree with the ideas in Sources **F** and **G**?

What was the legacy of the Cold War?

What are some of the long term 'costs' and benefits of the Great Power conflict? Has the Great Power conflict made the world a safer, or more dangerous, place? Which individuals, or movements, helped end the Great Power Conflict?

'The name's Bond ... James Bond'

You are growing up in the post Cold War era. Since it ended, Western images of the East have changed. Compare old 'James Bond' films with new ones. Old ones relied on old enemies – Soviet spies and Communist plots. Now, new 'arch villains' have had to be found.

Long-term problems

Yet, 45 years of Great Power conflict have left a range of long-term problems. These are shown, jumbled up, in the table opposite.

'Friends ... will be friends'

Despite the problems caused by the Great Power conflict, there is evidence of a new spirit of cooperation between former enemies. This may be seen through Source **A**.

Source A NASA space shuttle, Russian Mir space station. An astronaut space walks to repair faults, 1997

Long-term problems	
Nuclear weapons	In South East Europe bitter fighting between rival ethnic and religious groups led to mass killings.
Dangers of nuclear accidents	Nuclear weapon tests caused widespread radioactive contamination.
Nationalism	Problems remain for America in both Korea, where North Korea is Communist, and in Vietnam where the Communists took control. Many Americans still wonder, was their war worthwhile?
Cost	Incidents had happened in both America and Russia.
'Ethnic cleansing'	Its re-emergence led to calls for independence.
Environment	Billions were spend on defence systems, which could have been spent at home. Billions are now being spent to dismantle weapons.
SE Asia	Despite arms reductions, the three Great Powers maintained stockpiles of thousands of warheads.
Re-unification	To improve Russia's economy is a massive task. It will take Western help and will take many years to achieve.
Developing the Russian Federation	Fully uniting East and West Germany may take 20 years and will cost many billions per year.

Source **A** shows renewed cooperation between the Great Powers in space. Having arrived via a NASA space shuttle, an American astronaut assists a Russian cosmonaut to repair a damaged Russian space station.

A safer world

Has the Great Power conflict made the world a safer place? It is a matter of debate. Did *deterrence* work? Was it the fear of nuclear war which prevented it from happening? Before nuclear weapons there had been two World Wars. Since their arrival, there has been none. As Source **B** shows, both Great Powers have scaled down their armed forces in Europe.

Even so, the number of countries capable of developing nuclear weapons continues to *proliferate*. By 1997 some 20 countries had the capacity to threaten nuclear war, with the equivalent of 600,000 Hiroshima bombs. In 1997 a survey in the *Independent Sunday Review* revealed that the bookmakers, William Hill, offered the worst odds – at 500–1 – for the human race being wiped out by nuclear war.

Credit – where it's due

Casting aside such predictions, recall what you have already studied. Who are the individuals, or groups of people who have worked hardest – and have achieved the most – in bringing about an end to the Great Power conflict?

Stay aware ...

With a topic like the Great Power relations, some of the events you have studied are very recent. In fact, it is often difficult to say where 'history' stops and where 'news' or 'current affairs' begins. By the time you read this, new events concerning America, the Soviet Union and China will already have happened. Try to find out about them, and about what is happening at the moment, so that you can keep your knowledge of the Great Powers up-to-date.

Source B An ex-American air force base in Suffolk, opened in 1943, but then closed in response to the 'Peace Dividend'

The Great Power Conflict: a balloon game

■ The idea is to play a balloon game with the different people from the Cold War period. The aim is – briefly – to argue the case so that your character survives.

The characters in the basket are:
● Mikhail Gorbachev
● Lech Walesa
● Deng Xiaoping
● A Greenham Common woman
● Ronald Reagan
● An Anti–Vietnam War protester

■ Discuss in your group:
● what are your character's best qualities?
● you may expect your character to be attacked; prepare points to defend his/her reputation.
● prepare points against one or two other characters also in the balloon.

■ Remember, it's them or you who survive!

Questions

1 Study the table on page 92.
   a) On an enlarged copy of the table cut out the 'Problems' and 'Effects'.
   b) Match each pair of statements in the correct order.
   c) Re-order the pairs according to:
      i) time-span
      ii) importance.

2 Re-read 'A safer world'.
   a) Discuss whether nuclear weapons made a war between the Great Powers more or less likely during the Cold War.
   b) What is nuclear proliferation? What are some of its dangers?

3 Study the Great Power balloon game. Ask your teacher for full details to undertake this activity.

4 Think back to any recent world events involving Great Powers.
   a) Discuss what happened and which countries were involved.
   b) Did the event improve or worsen Great Power relations?

5 What sources of evidence could you use to write about a very recent event (in the last six months) involving the Great Powers?

6 What can you do to stay up-to-date with changes in Great Power conflict?

Glossary

A

Allies
People or countries who help each other, usually in time of war, or the threat of war.

Atom Bomb
A nuclear explosion of huge power, with long lasting side effects.

B

Biased
A one-sided version of events, giving or holding only one point of view.

'Bipolar'
The split in two, created by the Cold War, into the 'West' – led by America and the 'East' – led by the Soviet Union.

'Bloc'
A group of countries following a common interest or aim.

Blockade
To take hostile steps to stop supplies or equipment arriving at their destinations.

Boycott
To refuse to have anything to do with a country, often by not trading with its people.

'Breznev Doctrine'
Leonid Breznev's idea that all the Communist countries in Eastern Europe should behave according to the wishes of the Soviet Union.

'Brinkmanship'
The idea of testing one another's nerve in a major crisis to see which country 'backs down' first.

'Buffer Zone'
The countries of Eastern Europe which formed a buffer for the Soviet Union against possible invasion from the West.

C

Capitalism
The political and economic system which forms the basis of the 'West's' ideas. Property and businesses are privately owned – not by the state – and companies compete to make profits.

Cold War
The state of tension – stopping short of 'Hot War' – between the West (America and its Allies) and the East (the Soviet Union and its Communist allies).

Communism
A political and economic system which forms the basis of the East's ideas. The State, i.e. Communist Party, controls all aspects of life. (No private businesses or property exist.)

Containment
The attempt to keep a country's power within set limits and to stop it spreading any further.

D

Demilitarised
An area of land which, through agreements has no troops or weapons.

Democracy
A political system in which leaders representing different political parties are elected into power by citizens voting in regular elections The 'law making' body is a Parliament or Assembly.

Détente
A relaxation of tension, leading to cooperation between countries.

Deterrence
The idea of 'frightening off' possible enemies through their fear of the power of your own weapons.

Disarmament
Cutting down, or reducing the size of a country's store of troops and weapons.

Dissents
Individuals or groups who protest by speaking out against their nation's ideas and actions.

'Domino Theory'
The idea, held by America, that many countries in the Far East/SE Asia might quickly become Communist, unless America acted to prevent it.

E

Election
The process of electing a Government – or candidates – by choosing from a list of people through casting your vote.

Empire
A group of countries under the control of one ruler.

Encirclement
The idea of being surrounded, on all sides, by countries hostile to your own ways of life and ideas.

Escalate
To increase the amount of a country's war like actions against another.

'Ethnic Cleansing'
The idea of killing or driving out members of other races/religions from a mixed area to separate different ethnic groups into distinct areas.

G

Guerilla Warfare
The idea of fighting a larger, usually stronger and organised, army using surprise tactics. Guerillas are often

non-uniformed armed bandits, but share a fierce loyalty to their cause.

H
Hydrogen Bomb
A huge nuclear bomb many more times more powerful than an atomic bomb, with massively destructive effects.

I
Ideology
A particular view on the best way to run a country.

Independence
A wish to be free and not controlled by anyone else.

Inflation
Rapid rise in prices.

Interpretation
An explanation, or version, of motives, events and outcomes. Based on evidence, but coloured by the writer's attitudes and beliefs.

Imperialism
A political system in which a rich and powerful country controls other weaker countries.

Iron Curtain
The border between the East and West Europe. Built to stop the movement of people, and ideas, in 1946/47.

M
Martial Law
A situation where the Army takes over the running of a country.

Marxists
Followers of Karl Marx, the founder of ideas which developed into Communism.

Media
Newspapers, radio, TV, books, posters, pamphlets, films, etc.

N
Nationalism
A pride in one's own nation. A wish for it to be independent, in charge of its own destiny.

Non-Aligned Status
Countries, often in the Third World, who did not wish to take sides – neither 'East' nor 'West'.

P
Passive Resistance
The idea of protesting through non-cooperation in a 'non-violent' way.

Peaceful Co-existence
Khruschev's idea that East West could ease tensions by 'agreeing to disagree' with each others positions.

'Peace Dividend'
The idea that spending less on the arms race could lead to a rise in the standards of living.

Primary Evidence
Historical sources which are 'first-hand' – where the author was present or directly involved in the events described.

Propaganda
The idea of spreading false, or misleading information through the media to support a certain point of view.

Puppet Government
The idea of controlling a weak government, like a puppet, by a more powerful one.

R
Radiation
A feature of nuclear weapons which creates invisible rays leading to harmful effects.

Ratify
To approve.

Reparations
To offer, or demand, payments in compensation for damage.

S
Sanctions
A way of enforcing a decision against another country because of its actions.

Satellite
An object launched into space by a rocket to send back intelligence or act as a communication device. Also, a country under the control of a more powerful neighbour.

Secondary Evidence
A type of historical evidence based on first-hand accounts – but created by an author not directly involved or present at the events described.

'Sinatra Doctrine'
Gorbachev's idea that the former Soviet 'Satellites' should be allowed to 'make their own way' forward.

Spying
The process of gathering information about potential enemies.

Strategic Defence Initiative ('Star Wars')
Ronald Reagan's idea to protect America with a shield of laser-based weapons controlled from space satellites.

Summit Meeting
A meeting of world leaders.

Super Power
A very powerful country, with nuclear weapons, and during the Cold War. Different ideas on organising its country and peoples to best effect.

T
Third World
The poorer countries of the world, largely in Africa, Latin America and Asia. So named after the richer groups of countries in the First World (Capitalist) and Second World (Communist).

Treaty
A formal, written agreement to act as a country in an agreed way.

V
Veto
The power to stop, cancel or postpone a decision.

Index